HOOK UP, GET HIRED!
The Internet Job Search Revolution

JOYCE LAIN KENNEDY

JOHN WILEY & SONS, INC.
New York • Chichester • Brisbane • Toronto • Singapore

Cartoons were created by Ted Goff (74561.2632 @ compuserve.com)

Library of Congress Cataloging-in Publication Data:

Kennedy, Joyce Lain.
    Hook up, get hired! : the Internet job search revolution / Joyce
Lain Kennedy.
        p.   cm.
    Includes bibliographical references and index.
    ISBN 0-471-11629-7. — ISBN 0-471-11630-0 (pbk.)
    1. Job hunting—Data processing.   2. Internet (Computer network)
I. Title.
HF5382.7.K458   1995
650.14—dc20   94-48368

Printed in the United States of America

10 9 8 7 6 5 4 3 2

331.124
0 285
K458   7/96
1995

For

Eva June

Founder: National Council of Career Women
Founding Partner: Walling, June & Associates, Inc.

Executive recruiter Eva June Devries never cursed the darkness, but lit candles from Budapest to Washington. In July of 1994, she began a new state of being. Eva June was the most gallant woman her legions of friends have ever known. Salute!

TRADEMARKS AND USAGE OF COMPANY NAMES IN THIS BOOK

For readability, vendor names that appear in this work are not set in capital letters, nor are the signs indicating trademarks or service marks used. All known marks are listed below. This list is not necessarily complete. Any use of marked names, whether on this list or not, is editorial and to the benefit of the mark holder. The marks appear below as they are used by the companies holding the marks.

Mark	Appears in This Book as
Adobe™ Acrobat™ 　Adobe Systems	Acrobat
America Online℠ 　America Online, Inc.	AOL
CareerMosaic™ 　Bernard Hodes Advertising, Inc.	CareerMosaic
Common Ground™ Common Ground 　No Hands Software, Inc.	
CompuServe® Navigator 　CompuServe Incorporated	Navigator
Delphi™ 　DELPHI Internet Services Corporation	Delphi
DIALOG® 　© DIALOG Information Services	Dialog
Educators Online℠ Educators Online 　Executive Resource Associates, Inc.	
Enhanced NCSA Mosaic™ 　Spyglass, Inc.	Enhanced NCSA Mosaic
E-Mail Connection™ 　ConnectSoft	E-Mail Connection
Envoy™ 　WordPerfect® 　Novell Applications Group	Envoy
Eudora® 　QUALCOMM Incorporated	Eudora
eWorld® 　Apple Online Services	eWorld
GEnie® Aladdin 　General Electric Network for Information 　　Exchange	Aladdin
IBM PC® 　International Business Machines 　　Corporation	IBM PC
Job Bank USA™ 　Job Bank USA, Inc.	Job Bank USA
JobWeb™ 　National Association of Colleges 　　& Employers	JobWeb

Knowbot™ Knowbot Information Service	Knowbot
LEXIS®/NEXIS® Mead Data Central, Inc.	Lexis/Nexis
MCI® Mail MCI® Telecommunications Corporation	MCI Mail
MedSearch America™ MedSearch America, Inc.	MedSearch America
MKS® Internet Anywhere Mortice Kerns Systems, Inc.	MKS Internet Anywhere
NetCruiser™ Netcom On-Line Communication Services, Inc.	NetCruiser
Netscape™ Netscape Communications Corp.	Netscape
networkMCI Business™ MCI® Telecommunications Corporation	networkMCI Business
NewsNet® NewsNet, Inc.	NewsNet
Off-Line Xpress™ Mustang Software, Inc.	OLX
Pkware Pkware, Inc.	Pkware
ProComm Plus® DataStorm Technologies, Inc.	Procomm Plus
Prodigy® Prodigy Services Company	E-Mail Connection
QmodemPro for Windows™ Mustang Software, Inc.	QmodemPro
Replica™ Farallon Computing, Inc.	Replica
Remark trademark XXX Software Parners, Inc.	Remark
Slipknot™ MicroMind.Inc.	Slipknot
StuffIt Deluxe™ Aladdin Systems, Inc.	StuffIt
SuperPrint® Zenographics	SuperPrint
Transom™ Reach Media LP	Transom
The Well℠ Whole Earth 'Lectronic Link	The Well
Word® Microsoft	Word

Board of Advisers

These distinguished individuals served as advisers to this book, and have made excellent suggestions for its improvement. Any errors are solely the author's.

Andrew Barbour   Ottawa, Ontario, Canada
Author, *Recruiting in Cyberspace,* a master's degree research essay; human resource consultant, Price Waterhouse

Leo Charette   Williamsburg, Virginia
Director, Office of Career Services, College of William and Mary

Daniel P. Dern   Newton Center, Massachusetts
Author, *Internet Guide for New Users*

Susan Estrada   Carlsbad, California
Trustee, The Internet Society
CEO, NetPages directories/Aldea Communications, Inc.

Dr. Drema K. Howard   Lexington, Kentucky
Creator of *Jobplace,* a career development and job search discussion list for practitioners; University of Kentucky

Martin Kimeldorf   Tumwater, Washington
Author, *Workplace Journal* and *Educator's Job Search*

Harold L. Lemon   Union City, California
Author, *Harry's Job Search BBS* and *Internet Hot List*

Kenneth R. Milstead   Evanston, Illinois
Online Employment Resource Compiler

Steven J. Miller   Bethlehem, Pennsylvania
Director of Technology, National Association of Colleges and Employers

Jim Neumeister Charlottesville, Virginia
Technical Resources, Career Planning and Placement, University of Virginia

Debbie Nolan Reston, Virginia
Executive Director, The Internet Business Association

Nicholas Rench Topsfield, Massachusetts
CEO, Career Transition Network

Margaret F. Riley Worcester, Massachusetts
Circulation/Computer Resources Librarian, Gordon Library, Worcester
Polytechnic Institute

Dr. L. Patrick Scheetz East Lansing, Michigan
Career Development & Placement Services Assistant Director, Michigan
State University

Jerry Whelan Calverton, New York
Network Programmer, Brookhaven National Laboratory

Tom Wills San Mateo, California
Internet Consultant

Foreword

The Internet, in'ter · net *n.* [Prefix *inter,* between, and *net* cog. L, *nassa* a basket for catching fish]—A world-wide community that electronically links leading-edge thinkers and ordinary people, government and business, the world's leading universities and high schools, job hunters and employers . . . . With tens of millions of members, one of the world's most powerful "clubs." Begun in 1968 as a U.S. Defense Department project. Syn. Cyberspace. The Information Highway. The Net. The Web. Also see: America Online, CompuServe, GEnie, Delphi, Prodigy, Pipeline.

Read my definition of the Internet and think of the power of sitting at your own home computer or office PC and accessing current job listings—the federal and local governments, insurance, construction management, MIS, sales, accounting, training and development, entertainment and media are only some of the fields.

Openings may be found for economists, software engineers, librarians, teachers, and others around the country—or around the world. Sound pretty good? You might go a step further tying into a *Young Scientists Network*—a group of about 4,000 white-collar scientists linked together with one mission in mind: sharing information about career opportunities. Too good to be true? A few years ago, maybe.

What would you think about gaining access to annual reports for *every* public company in America? Or to real-time industry information to help you plan your next career? What about articles on how to write a resume and an attention-getting cover letter? Do you need expert advice on how to prepare for an interview? Would a database of entry-level salaries help you to measure your market value? Would you be interested in databanks that will carry your resume, so companies looking for someone with your credentials can seek *you* out?

It's all there, and more! To press your imagination a little further, there are even guided tours through The White House in Washington and the Louvre in Paris, complete with music and pictures. You can take French lessons from French Public Radio, or order your own custom version of a favorite daily newspaper to read with your morning coffee. Soon, you'll be able to access the entire Library of Congress—right from your home or office.

The good news is that today's computers and virtual push-button technology make getting on the Net as simple as 1-2-3.

The real challenge—and a key advantage—of the Internet is its sheer size. There's a lot of prediction in the press lately about future television-viewer confusion in choosing among 500 channels. Consider the fact that the Internet *currently* links more than 5 million host machines (read channels) and provides connectivity to literally tens of thousands of BBSs, or bulletin board systems (read networks). Rather than testing your technological savvy, cyberspace tests the ways you access, use, communicate, and organize information.

Hook Up. Joyce Lain Kennedy's earlier books—*Electronic Job Search Revolution* and *Electronic Resume Revolution*—really help job hunters (and their mentors) develop the understanding and skills needed to exploit fundamental changes in how America's human resource departments have reengineered and automated their hiring functions. *Hook Up, Get Hired!* takes you to the next logical step toward a whole new world of "Emerald Icebergs" and "Wild Blue Cyberspace"—*the Internet*.

Importantly, Joyce Lain Kennedy leverages her knowledge as one of the nation's leading career and job-search experts to the advantage of her reader. *Hook Up, Get Hired!* isn't just another book about the Internet; neither is it a book about technology. Rather, it is the first complete job search book that eases the reader—whether a computer novice or an expert—through the technospeak of connectivity, and the maze of the Internet, to unparalleled employment resources. This book reveals:

- How to find current job postings online, and how to respond;
- How to post your resume—formatted for the Internet medium;
- How to electronically research a company, and prepare for an interview;
- How to network with others who share your interest;
- How to plan your career and seek expert advice.

Hook Up, Get Hired! is carefully organized and includes dozens of case studies of real-life searches. References help you tailor access to your own particular needs, technical capacities, AND budgets. Each chapter is presented in an easily digestible manner with step-by-step guideposts that allow anyone to "Just Do It!"

For better jobs and career management, read this book, then try the Internet for a weekend. You'll never look back.

MICHAEL R. FORREST
Executive Director
National Association of Colleges and Employers
(Formerly the College Placement Council)
michael@jobweb.org

Bethlehem, Pennsylvania
March 1995

The National Association of Colleges and Employers is a not-for-profit association established in 1956 to support the efforts of college career services representing more than 90 percent of today's higher education students, and employer recruitment professionals.

Thanks a Million

As the Three Tenors—José Carreras, Plácido Domingo and Luciano Pavarotti—are to music, these Four Aces are to me.

Eduardo N. Guevara, Jr., who, at age 17, is graduating from Carlsbad (California) High School as this book is being published. My technical editorial associate and chief researcher, Ed's career goal is to advance from summer intern Internaut to United States Astronaut. Ed's right stuff will make it happen.

Muriel W. Turner, a.k.a. Wonder Woman. Muriel gave up retirement to pull me out of a landfill of paper bits, written pieces, and published loose ends related to this book. Without her expert help, I would still be mired in a forest of wood chips and looking for a mulcher. Thanks, Muriel, my pal.

Steve Eisenberg, a professional technical consultant, tested and retested more online software than I ever knew existed. Steve also ran the Internet roads searching for places to job shop, called to my attention late-breaking developments, and straightened me out on numerous technical issues. Merci, Steve!

Laura Ruekberg, an industrial-strength editor and personal friend whose editorial gifts shine through in this book. Today's rapidly changing technology makes writing about it akin to chasing a moving target while trying to leap aboard a speeding train. Laura, who put a rocket on my motor, has my enduring gratitude.

J.L.K.

Acknowledgments

There are many individuals who deserve special mention for the numerous ways they helped during the creation and production of this book:

- At John Wiley & Sons:
  Stephen A. Kippur, Senior Vice President, Professional, Reference and Trade Group; **Jeffrey W. Brown,** Executive Publisher; **Mike Hamilton,** Senior Editor; and **Mary Daniello,** Associate Managing Editor.

- At Publications Development Corporation:
  Maryan Malone and **Nancy Marcus Land.**

- At Sun Features, Inc.:
  Marianne D. Horrell and **Tomer Verona.**

- For the Cartoons:
  Ted Goff (74561.2632@compuserve.com).

- For numerous consults:
  Regina Aulisio, Consultant; **Patrick O'Leary,** Consultant; and **James M. Lemke,** Consultant.

J.L.K.

NetNote

Terms to Know

Online refers to electronic exchanges of information by computers, telephone lines, cable, or network services.

Information highway refers to a yet-to-be-built cable and telephone-line network that will allow consumers to access massive amounts of information directly from their homes and offices.

The Internet is a precursor to the information highway, but in popular media the terms are being used interchangeably.

Cyberspace is a term coined by William Gibson in his fantasy novel, *Neuromancer,* to describe the "world" of computers and the society that gathers around them.

Virtual means a system that simulates real life. It's a word that has come to mean computer-related to something familiar, such as a virtual corporation.

Contents

contracts. Meet some of the people who already are on the roadway, and watch out for employment scams.

3   Information Highway Trip Tickets   31

Like the trip tickets you order from auto clubs before a journey, here is what every job seeker must know about the Internet's resources and organizing systems—including points of interest and decent places to stay, plus a lineup of online management tools that keep you on course and propel you to your destination.

4   JOBS Looking for People   53

*Here's what you've been waiting for—the places where
employers post jobs. From commercial job banks to informal,
chatty groups. From corporate America to the U.S.
government. The Internet's a splendid source for finding the
job you've always wanted.*

5   PEOPLE Looking for Jobs   121

*A sampling of the kinds of databases that employers and
recruiters search when they're on the prowl for resumes.
They may be recruiting for jobs right now . . . or window
shopping for gleam-in-the-eye positions. Update your
information interviewing efforts by networking on the Net.*

6   CyberOpportunities for Small Business   137

*Looking for something other than a nine-to-five job? Use
the Internet to land consulting stints . . . find freelance
assignments . . . work from home . . . market your own
business . . . move around the globe.*

7   Where Do I Start? (And Where's the Panic Button?)   153

*Are you ready to make the right connections? Here are
answers to basic questions, and a few special technical tips
to readers who are playing the job market. Remember, when
in doubt, log out.*

8   Put Your Job Search on Autopilot   171

*The impatient or thrifty job hunter can turn to a variety of
high octane shortcuts—from macros to offline readers. Will
one of these e-helpers make you more efficient at finding a job?*

9 Job Finding Strategies and Savvy Moves   193

*Managing your work and life in ways new to our times puts
you in front of the competition. Here are a few bonus points
to make you a frequent winner.*

Appendix: The Scenic Tour   215

Resources That Show You the Best Ways to Go around the Net

Glossary   229

Information Highway Terms Made Simple

Index   241

Introduction

Emerald Icebergs and Wild Blue Cyberspace:
Solving the Mysteries

Scientists have finally solved the secret of the emerald icebergs sighted from ships navigating the waters of Antarctica.

For centuries in a land of savage winds and plummeting temperatures, the wind-sculpted green spires of ice spiking on the horizon were a puzzlement. For eons, only polar creatures like emperor penguins, crabeater seals, and snow petrels stood sentry over the immense green pyramids of ice that sometimes appeared amid the white chunks ripped from the great Antarctic icecap.

When the ancient mariners in their multimasted schooners came to take a look around, they could only wonder *what the green pyramids might be*. Meteorites rained down from a place beyond human reach? Ooze, razor-sharp and petrified, jutting from the ocean's floor? An intensely green variety of a mirage-like phenomenon known as iceblink—unseen ice fields below the horizon, reflected against a frosty overcast sky?

Because icebergs' submerged parts may tear open a ship, they are difficult to approach—especially in the inhospitable climate of isolated Antarctica. Even modern, better-equipped explorers in thick steel-hulled ships didn't quickly unravel the green enigma.

Finally, the veils of the mystery were lifted. A new scientific explanation was offered and it was less mind-boggling than perplexed ship captains might have expected. An emerald iceberg, according to a new study, is nothing more than your everyday iceberg turned upside down, like a capsized ship.

Why is it rich in the color green? The emerald showpieces, scientists say, broke loose from huge slabs of frozen snow called ice shelves, which have a blue tint. Yellow-toned organic matter—algae and plankton, for example—sticks to the bottom of the ice shelves. It takes hundreds of years for the yellow shading to develop.

When the iceberg flips upside down, the color yellow sitting atop the color blue, becomes visible. As any finger-painting kid knows, yellow and blue make green. Mystery solved!

The icy emerald mystery reminds me of another giant question that is on the minds of millions of people around the world: the wild blue cyberspace. People everywhere have heard about computers linking together, but many don't understand the nature of the hookup.

HELP FOR THE TECHNOLOGICALLY CHALLENGED

While alert, ambitious people have heard about computers being used to form a gigantic and comprehensive web—*cyberspace*—most are wondering how to get in the cyberspace game.

(The technical view is more precise, but in the street definition, cyberspace means the universe made possible by a huge network of computers hooked together.)

The *Internet, going online,* the *information highway,* the *data highway*—every day, people are hearing these and other references to the cyberspace thing. They aren't too sure about the differences. They'd like to get in on the cutting-edge technology but haven't learned how to even begin to crack the cyberspace mystery.

Just as most mariners once were perplexed by sightings of the strange emerald icebergs in the Antarctic waters, most landlubbing Internet newbies are positively stupefied at the thought of the technologically mysterious components of the wild blue cyberspace.

Technology novices fear the unknown. They wonder: Cyberspace— what is it? What on earth happens when "those computers" join a gigantic electronic jamboree?

Even those who aren't apprehensive of things technical may be apathetic about conquering change. Word people and liberal arts types (the author is one) worry about how long it's going to take before they can gain the skills to crawl, much less walk, in cyberspace. Mastery seems light years beyond them. And the language on the Internet! To a liberal arts mind, techies talk funny. They "reconfigure," they run "TCP/IP" software on the "LAN," they achieve "connectivity"—they communicate in terms that don't mean much to ordinary mortals. The curious customs of Net veterans seem designed to keep rookies in the ditches alongside the information highway.

I used to wonder about the wild blue cyberspace myself. Last year, when I decided the time had come to smarten up, I timidly approached the Net and became a "newbie," or new arrival. Only recently have I moved up a notch from Net-newbieness, after spending months cruising the electronic highways as flame bait, all in the name of journalistic research.

My experiences led to two conclusions. First, like the emerald icebergs, cyberspace isn't so frightening once you start seriously looking into it. Familiarity breeds confidence.

Taming the wild blue cyberspace doesn't require a whip and a chair. Instead, you need the determination not to miss out on one of history's most exciting times—good times that are just beginning. As a project, job hunting in cyberspace is doable.

The second conclusion is that, as is the case with emerald icebergs, hidden perils lurk beneath the surface—perils that could sink your electronic ship if you just throw your resume onto the Net and hope for the best.

YOUR GUIDE TO JOB FINDING ON THE INTERNET

What you're reading now will give you just enough hands-on instruction to hop on the Net and speed along, but not so much that you're overwhelmed and need a nap.

Without this beginner's map to a new universe, your resume may land in places that employers never visit. If you're a manager, you don't want to post to a bulletin board that specializes in finding baby sitters. In addition, you may miss the job postings that are appropriate for you. If you're a physical therapist, you don't want to waste time reading job postings for software engineers.

Even with this beginner's map, you may get lost on the information highway for any number of reasons, including "pilot errors" that are up to you to correct. Or you may get lost because a resource has moved and your message bounces back with no forwarding electronic address.

NetNote

A Hot Time Online

A flame is a verbal conflagration, a piece of mail or a general message that is rudely argumentative. Flamers yell at you on screen for what they consider dimbo mistakes, such as posting messages in the wrong places or behaving without appropriate reverence for the Net culture as they perceive it.

When I went out on the Internet with requests that people share their job stories, I was both flamed and applauded.

I burned the former and laminated the latter.

(At press time, all job resources in this book had been checked several times for accuracy; however Internet job hunting is a dynamic new trend: resources regularly appear and disappear. Moreover, addresses are being changed with the speed of light, particularly on the World Wide Web.)

If you are a clueless beginner who is scared stiff of computers, will this book make you a computer-literate online job hunter? Sorry, the answer is no. That task is beyond the scope of this work.

What this book will do is give you targeted job-finding information not elsewhere available.

Technically speaking, this book will stand you firmly on square one facing forward. If I've done my job right, you will be actively interested in finding out more through continuing education classes, computer tutors, general computer/Internet books, and other resources. Many opportunities to become Internet-literate are available.

KEEP YOUR EYE ON THE JOB BALL

Hook Up, Get Hired! answers job-related questions. It does not replay the numerous step-by-step, hand-holding, expansive, and often excellent guides on general techniques for finding your way around the Internet.

Until you solve your personal career issues, whatever they may be, my advice is: **Focus on the job hunt itself.** For now leave the finer points of trying to hitch a ride into cyberspace to people who have technology sense. To me this quality is like perfect pitch: You either have it, or you don't.

Later on, you can become as technically expert as you like. At this point, don't worry too much if you are technologically uninitiated. *Believe me: If I can effectively operate machines of cosmic significance in a job search, you can too, even when the mere thought of technology gives you a four-aspirin headache.*

My initial solution was to hire a smart teenager who could demystify cyberspace complexities. Had I not been able to pay, I would have had to adopt him—he was that valuable. Later, I added a seasoned technical consultant to the book's team. When this work was almost completed, still another young computer wizard came aboard. I had the advantage of having three technical specialists available; you can find similar start-up help if you make the effort.

You'll be glad you did. Someone has said that learning to get around on the information highway is like driving a car for the first time after having grown up riding a bike. You learn to go faster with less effort.

This book, describing the methods of online and Internet job hunting, joins my two other volumes in the Wiley job market revolution trilogy:

Electronic Job Search Revolution and *Electronic Resume Revolution,* both of which were written with coauthor Thomas J. Morrow.

Electronic Job Search Revolution reports critical trends that are changing the employment process: the use of computers to screen applicants, the availability of employer databases in various fields, and artificial intelligence software that allow job hunters to practice their job interviewing skills.

Electronic Resume Revolution shows how to write computer-friendly resumes that keep you competitive in an era of evolving employment technology, whether the resume is to be transmitted on paper or by e-mail or fax.

As you contemplate the wild blue cyberspace stretching ahead, remember the lesson of the emerald icebergs: It's a lot easier to get to the bottom of things than it might once have seemed.

If you already are computer-competent and are looking at this book because you know there are jobs out there and you want some of them but just don't know where to look, head straight for the steroids of job search resources in Chapter 4.

AN OVERVIEW

Here is what this book covers, chapter by chapter.

- **Chapter 1**—an overview of the new power triad in the job search process: (1) print materials and traditional third-party employment services; (2) personal, one-on-one contacts; and (3) the electronic universe, especially Internet activities. The Internet offers new help for midlife job hunters, and the launching of *JobWeb* is making prospects brighter for the college crowd. It isn't necessary to move out of town for jobs you're likely to find online, but there are clear indications that a global job market is evolving.

- **Chapter 2**—a collection of true Internet employment experiences, and a warning about junk ads you may see online.

- **Chapter 3**—the resources you must know to "work the Net," such as bulletin boards, newsgroups, discussion lists, Gopher Jewels, World Wide Web, and more.

- **Chapter 4**—a wide-angled presentation of specific resources you can use to find jobs. In some cases, you can also post your resume. Includes permanent, temporary, full- and part-time, and contract jobs. Contains the most comprehensive online directory in print.

- **Chapter 5**—additional specific resources that identify how people look for jobs and network on the Net. Includes suggestions for applicants seeking permanent, temporary, full- and part-time, and contract jobs. Advice is given on information interviewing in cyberspace, a new lease on an old strategy.

- **Chapter 6**—small business and other entrepreneurial avenues to success in cyberspace that do not require a nine-to-five career path. Real-life stories show how paid work and job hunters can come together in fields that range from consulting and freelance writing to mom-and-pop marketing activities and contract opportunities. Executive recruiters now share business openings and interact on the information highway.

- **Chapter 7**—a primer chapter on the basic steps that technically uninitiated job seekers must take to launch a job search on the Internet. Plain instructions are given on how to send resumes and cover letters online, as well as a report on new technology that makes it easier than ever before.

- **Chapter 8**—"autopilots." These new ideas and software can save job seekers time, money, or frustration when they post or e-mail resumes to many employers or to targeted employers. Includes tips on how to get on and off the Internet quickly and painlessly.

- **Chapter 9**—new strategies and techniques to uncover opportunities through skills searching, and online netiquette. They, in turn, lead to more savvy moves that are discovered as computer screens light up with jobs.

Let's begin our great adventure in cyberspace, which may turn out to be the voyage of a lifetime.

Job Finding: The Internet Family Connections

1

Internet! . . . The information highway! . . . Cyberspace!
The exploding electronic universe means finding a job
will never be the same. Job hunters, now you can be
everywhere at once!

THE HOTTEST HIRING TREND OF THE 1990s

The Texan in this story has first-hand experience with the settling of the electronic frontier. Bruce Brazell well understands that epochal change is taking place as jobs and people reach out for each other by hooking computers to a big hiring hall in the incredible cybersky.

In what is no less than a new power triad for job finding, paper is not history, and personal contacts are not in the Ice Age. Both are as essential as ever. But a third leg has been added to the job hunting structure: electronics. The electronic dimension began with job computers and databases and is rushing forward in the salons of cyberspace.

As you read this book, job seekers and employers are signaling each other in the chatty corridors of *computer bulletin boards,* the more structured hallways of *online services,* and countless other discussion rooms in the edifice of electronic connections that is the *Internet.*

Bruce Brazell, an educator in astronomy, didn't need the Hubble Space Telescope to figure out what was happening in cyberspace. He well understood that the world of jobs and the chances of latching on to them are changing. Brazell hit the Internet. Celestially speaking, it was a good decision.

Brazell moved last year from high school science teacher to planetarium director. He also moved halfway across the country, with his wife, two sons, one daughter, one dog, and one cat. At the end of the star trek: the directorship of the Alice G. Wallace Planetarium in Fitchburg, Massachusetts.

A 1991 graduate of West Texas A&M in physics, Brazell had spent nearly three years teaching high school science and studying for a master's degree in astronomy, when, one day in May, Brazell decided it was a fine time to think about the future. He fired up his 386 PC, which held a 2400-baud modem, and cruised the Internet through the Texas Educators Network, an educators' free online service.

Originally, Brazell says, he was "poking around" the Net scouting a job for his wife, who was interested in teaching history or working at a museum. "Just for fun I typed in 'planetarium' to see if anything popped to the screen. I found the planetarium job—it had been listed that same day!"

After mailing the requisite resume and cover letter, a month passed before Brazell was interviewed by telephone and invited to come north for a face-to-face interview. He was the last candidate to be seen. The job offer came in June, immediately after the interview.

How had the planetarium job posting found its way to the Internet in the first place? David A. Davidowicz, an entrepreneur whom you'll meet later in this book, learned about the position vacancy and did the planetarium a favor by posting it online.

The planetarium search committee had no idea the vacancy had been zapped across the nation electronically. "They were totally amazed," Brazell chuckles. "The other 47 applications, all from people in the local area, had come in the standard way of newspaper job ads and word-of-mouth messages. Then, out of the blue, here comes a resume from a guy in Texas!"

The information highway is changing not only the way people work, but the way people get work. If you are not wired into cyberspace, it's time to find out what you're missing. Depending on your line of work, you could be missing quite a lot.

The third leg of the employment process—electronics, including on-line job search—is just as sturdy as the two other legs: the *traditional job search,* including print recruitment ads and third-party employment services, and *personal contact,* including the one-on-one communication that has made networking a buzzword and is a widely practiced job search method.

The new kid in the employment triad, electronics, is rapidly establishing its turf among people who did not grow up with computers, and people who have become famous for their personal touch.

It is very difficult to outnetwork the nation's premier networker, Harvey Mackay, whose bestselling books, speeches, and media appearances extol the virtues of personal networking.

In his nationally syndicated newspaper column, Mackay recently dealt with electronic job search. He wrote that he often hears about people sending out 300 resumes and not getting a single response:

> It's a problem I run into everywhere I go. I thought I had the answer: "Customize your resume. Concentrate on one target at a time. Differentiate yourself from the pack. Demonstrate your knowledge of that employer and your fit with their corporate culture."
>
> Not bad, but . . . I can do better now: **Don't send out 500 resumes. Send out 100,000 resumes.**

Mackay was talking about using electronic databases and searching online.

Ready or not, your job hunt is about to change. The information revolution has already begun to work its wonders, as Bruce Brazell found when he climbed a digital stairway to the stars.

HELLO WORLD!

She's only five years old, but precocious Megan McLaughlin of La Costa, California already has the right take on the world phenomenon called the Internet, the forerunner of the evolving information highway.

Hearing that Megan had learned about cyberspace from her parents, who are Internet gurus, a well-meaning adult visitor asked Megan if she was excited about the coming information revolution. "With computers, you can play games, but with the Internet, you'll be able to play with kids in Spain or France, or many other places. Isn't that gonna be great?," the nice lady asked.

Flashing her winsome smile, Megan looked straight at the woman and shot back, "I can do that now. The Internet isn't a gonnabe, it's an isabe."

Wise beyond her years, Megan may even sense that humankind is poised to go boldly where no society has gone before: deep into cyberspace, where the electronic dimension is fundamentally changing the way people think, communicate with each other, do business, and find jobs.

The fastest growing communications medium in history, the Internet is unquestionably the new frontier where jobs and people are teaming up to make money, or make a difference—or both. In just a few years, 100 million computers will be performing on the Internet stage.

Electronic prospects are so phenomenal that even traditional print media are joining the "e-club." Major newspapers and magazines now include regular online sections, such as Newsweek's Cyberscope page, or put their entire publication online as do *U.S. News & World Report* and *Time.* An anonymous commentator summed it up: The Internet quite simply is the biggest communications advance since Johann Gutenberg took printed words out of the abbey.

So big, in fact, that home computer sales jumped last year by nearly 7 million machines, 40 percent of all the personal computers sold in the U.S. The PC is rapidly becoming, in the words of *Business Week,* "Mr. and Mrs. North America's on-ramp to the Information Superhighway. PCs, not TVs, are becoming the 'platform' for delivering all sorts of new digital products and services—from online magazines . . . to virtual classrooms."

Although only a small percentage of computer owners have hooked up to a network in the past, industry observers are nearly unanimous in predicting the connectivity rate will burst its seams within the next couple of years. The reasons: intense competition for customers is resulting in lowered online prices, commercial online services are making it easier every day to travel to and fro on the Net, and new computers are being packaged with built-in Internet access.

Another reason, and not the least important, is the general public's growing awareness of the Internet and its possibilities. A study last year, the *American Information User Survey*[1], found that more than 50 percent of its sample 2,000 households strongly agreed that computers can be very helpful and that "new ways of sending and receiving information electronically are good for the environment." More than 60 percent

[1]FIND/SVP, a New York-based research and consulting firm; 1994.

strongly agreed that "new electronic information systems are critical to improve the educational system in our country."

Compared to the general populace, small business owners are only gradually discovering the Net. A study last year, *Small Business and the Information Superhighway,*[2] showed that most small business owners have heard of the "information superhighway," and sense that it ultimately will be a business asset. The details remain fuzzy, with only one-quarter of respondents claiming their Internet knowledge rates from "a fair amount to a lot."

Because of massive advertising campaigns offering communications packages that combine such things as discount telephone service, e-mail, videoconferencing, and information highway services, great numbers of small businesses are now likely to wake up to the Internet and realize, "If we're not there, we may not be anywhere."

As we begin our study of how the Internet can infuse job searches and career management needs with new vigor, the first thing to understand is that the Internet isn't a thing. It isn't a corporation or an organization. No one owns it. No one runs it. The Internet is simply everyone's computers all hooked up together.

If you're not yet convinced of its importance, read what *Fortune* magazine has said: "Internet will be as essential as water, power, phones, sewers, roads—and beer."

THE TRUE-OR-FALSE NET QUIZ

How savvy are you about the Internet? Make a true-false choice for these questions before you read the answers that follow.

	True	False
1. More men than women surf the Internet.	_____	_____
2. Most people on the Net are young.	_____	_____
3. Most opportunities on the Net are technical jobs.	_____	_____
4. You will have to relocate as a result of job hunting on the Net.	_____	_____
5. Using newspapers to job hunt will no longer be necessary.	_____	_____
6. Personal live networking eventually will become obsolete.	_____	_____

[2]International Business Machines Corp. study conducted by Roper Starch Worldwide Inc.; 1994.

	True	**False**
7. You can learn Internet skills at libraries and continuing education programs, as well as in high schools and colleges.	_____	_____
8. Those who are not computer literate are in danger of having their careers overtaken by technology.	_____	_____
9. The Internet makes it easier to change jobs when the boss is looking.	_____	_____
10. The Internet may be able to improve employment opportunities for people with disabilities.	_____	_____

Answers

1. *True.* Of a handful of studies, none are statistically without challenge, but all have come to the same general conclusions. For example, two recent studies, one by the Massachusetts Institute of Technology (MIT) and the other by researchers at the Georgia Institute of Technology (GIT), confirm that Internet users buy their clothing in the men's department. The MIT study showed that nearly 87 percent of I-way users are male; the GIT study of the World Wide Web produced even more lopsided results: 94 percent are male.

A Canadian study, *Recruiting in Cyberspace,* by Andrew G. Barbour, an adviser to this book, confirms that participation in Internet recruiting—at least for information systems personnel—is chiefly male. Barbour notes that the low proportion of females (15% in his study) could be a problem if an organization has an "equity program in place and has targeted the information systems function as an area for improvement."

A number of other studies and observations agree that women are not plugged into power networks. Reasons vary from the pipeline problem of women just recently beginning to pursue technical majors, to a general lack of mentors to light the murky paths into cyberspace. A popular joke line is that "a technical female is an oxymoron."

Women must overcome one distasteful set of hurdles: the politically incorrect remarks men sometimes fire at them in a kind of "Power Ranger vs. Barbie" exchange.

In a particularly lurid instance, a private message degenerated into a man's request for a woman's sexual preferences. Deciding enough is enough, the woman put a stop to the harassment with a simple message: "I've only got two words for you, and they're not 'happy birthday.'"

Much of today's rough I-way culture will change as larger numbers of women enter the electronic frontierland and show they have the true grit of their ancestors, the pioneer women who helped tame frontiers in the West and in outer space.

The gender gap is almost certain to shrink. Bombarded by advertising and media blurbs about the information age, women are daily becoming more aware of the potential of the Internet to smooth their lives in a multitude of ways, ranging from finding jobs to home shopping—and they are beginning to teach their daughters the importance of using electronic tools to build their future.

2. *True.* The MIT study showed that Internet users, in general, have an average age of 31 years; the GIT study reported an age range of 21 to 30 years. These age group findings did not directly correspond with my experience in researching this book. I communicated with large numbers of people on the Net who, evident from their own stories, will never see 35 again. The difference may show up when my subject matter, jobs, is compared to the entire scope of Internet topics, which is as broad as an encyclopedia's.

3. *True.* I could not find studies supporting the presumption that most jobs posted on the Internet are technical in nature and are particularly concentrated in data processing and management information systems. Almost every one of the hundreds of people with whom I communicated, however, made that assertion.

This occupational demographic, too, is changing rapidly. Almost 100 percent of the people I interviewed agreed that the online job market is opening to nontechnical personnel.

As one professor explained, "One of the primary problems you have in finding humanities students [for this book] is their previous lack of Internet access. At our university, engineering and physical science students have been hooked to the Net for years. Every student in these curricula is given an account upon enrollment and is free to use it without time restrictions.

"Humanities students are just now getting access to the system [fall of 1994]. Now all students have access."

4. *False.* Because the Internet and other online services bring the world much closer, many searchers think that only out-of-town jobs can be found through electronic job search.

Not so. The surge of freenets (see Chapter 3), which turns a community into a big electronic grapevine; the tidal wave of computer bulletin boards, many of which are filled with local job and resume listings; and the local newsgroups all provide a means of looking for work in your own backyard.

Mike Chaney, a software engineer in Washington, DC, changed jobs with an online search: "Using keywords, I found a job that really fit my criteria. I didn't have to do the hard [search] work because the keywords filtered out the jobs that weren't suited for me. I really found what I was looking for," says Chaney. "The job was described to a T, and it fit so perfectly I didn't even have to relocate."

5. *False*. Newspapers—their news and their recruitment ads—continue to be vital resources in a transitional era. Newspapers themselves are moving to place online not only their employment ads, but their entire publications. As the Newspaper Association of America's Ira Gordon observes:

"After years of reporting the implications of the infobahn, virtually dozens of newspaper companies are starting to travel it. They are leveraging their editorial, information, and advertising strengths, creating online extensions of the printed product, new services for advertisers, and potential new revenue streams."

The *New York Times,* for example, is testing the practicality of making its help-wanted classifieds available, via Gopher, Telnet, and World Wide Web, to everyone on the Internet (see Chapter 3).

The *Atlanta Journal & Constitution* has linked up with Prodigy, a commercial online service, and others are following, including the *Los Angeles Times.*

Electronic job hunters are delighted to be able to save time by calling up the electronic classified ads, typing in the occupations of interest, and seeing only listings of interest to them.

Some trailblazing newspapers are operating online centers, such as the *San Jose Mercury* News's Mercury Center. With a PC and modem, you can get classified ads, archived *Mercury News* articles, weather, movie schedules, sports, messaging, and stock prices.

Newspapers are here to stay, although the communications format is being reexamined for possible marketing line extensions through the new media. "Interactive services developers will seek alliances with newspapers who command the business—who have the largest databases—whether it's classified, entertainment, or financial. Newspapers are in the enviable position of becoming content providers, where much of the action is going to be, as the search for profitable interactive services intensifies," Gordon explains.

6. *False*. Live networking will never be obsolete, but the Internet multiplies your opportunities exponentially. The principles of self-marketing won't change either. Instead of a posting that reads "I need a job, does anyone out there know of one?," your approach should be the same as in a traditional search, "I am a specialist in [whatever] and am ready for the next step up."

7. *True.* Libraries and learning institutions everywhere are launching Internet study opportunities, from workshops to courses. Attending a group session is a good way to break in: You won't be alone in asking "dumb" questions.

8. *True.* World commerce is on the cusp between yesterday and tomorrow. The West no longer has dibs on sophisticated high-tech jobs. In the United States, even the best-trained workers are facing stiff foreign competition. One correspondent to this book complained that some contract employment services are bypassing U.S. computer programmers, to whom they would have to pay $35 or $40 an hour, and hiring overseas programmers at $5 to $15 an hour.

As training and experience in less developed countries rapidly improve, the West's technologically unprepared workers may find themselves on the bicycle lanes of the information highway. Fast-lane travelers will be those who know how to manage money and technology.

Anyone who doesn't want to work a lot cheaper had better learn to work a lot smarter.

9. *True.* Looking for a job without the boss finding out and expediting your departure was never easy, and it isn't now. But it can be done honestly and discreetly. Don't use your company's equipment after hours. You can go online to research at home, or use copy shops that rent computers, photocopy machines, printers, and fax facilities. Remember that many potential employers are turned off when they see you have used your current employer's equipment (e-mail headers show the source, for instance). As mentioned elsewhere in this book, posting your resume for the world to see and networking your intentions to leave can be risky. Decide whether you need to disguise your name and identifiable company names on your resume. You may want to ask that employer responses be sent to a friend, or to commercial online career firms that offer confidential service.

10. *True.* The Internet offers not only opportunities to scout for jobs on a level playing field, but special services for people with disabilities. Substantial research on the issue is beyond the scope of this book, but a bulletin board system in Sweden is an example.

Operated by the Swedish Society for the Deaf and Blind, e-mail and conferencing systems are used to facilitate recruitment and job placement.

Score

If you correctly answered at least three of the above questions, you are entitled to wear one of those cute little beanies with a propeller on top. You are now a propeller head with a good chance of flying through cyberspace.

LIFE AFTER A JOBLESS 50TH BIRTHDAY

The downsizing frenzy has turned life upside down for hundreds of thousands of workers in their 40s, 50s, and 60s, who became accustomed to the expansive era that followed World War II. They worked under a set of rules that rewarded loyalty and performance with job security.

Those rules are in the ditch. A person who counts on company loyalty today is a person ripe for disappointment.

Here's what one displaced midlifer, or "middie," wrote to me for inclusion in my newspaper column (Los Angeles Times Syndicate), *Careers:*

> Dear Joyce:
>
> I became jobless at 50, after 34 years at the same company. I was in the job market for one year. To say the transition was difficult on me mentally, financially, and otherwise would not begin to tell the story. . . . If you think you are lost, unprepared for the next day, feel betrayed, angry at the system, and are too old to begin again, you are in good company.

I've read similar sentiments from middie after middie. So has the American Association of Retired Persons. In their informal study, which included 10,000 members, the message came through loud and clear. Most displaced middies think their dismissals violated the Age Discrimination in Employment Act, and midlife workers are feeling the squeeze of broken promises.

The obvious question is: "Can the new Internet search techniques really offer middies a bright blue cyberscape, or is the Net just new packaging for old hot air?" There's reason to hope the answer is "Yes, the Internet can help repair lives," once people who did not grow up with computers get over their technophobia and learn how to get around on the I-way.

To explain my reasoning, here are just three of the job search rites that can be made more accessible, speeded up, or vastly expanded by using Internet resources:

1. **Making a career choice**
   You can use the Net either to reaffirm that you want to stay in the type of work you've been doing, or to decide to make a change. Interest inventories, a type of self-quiz, are available online; use them to help figure out what you *like to do*. Skills inventories are also available; use them to focus on what you *can do*. Both kinds of inventories are available in the career concentration sections of commercial online services.

2. **Locating job openings**
   You can search locally, or cast a wider, faraway net—by using computerized bulletin boards, freenets, newsgroups, and mailing lists (see Chapters 3 and 4). Other job hunters can give you tips about the process of job hunting and leads to job vacancies they didn't want; the openings may interest you.

3. **Boosting morale**
   Self-esteem takes a nosedive when you're put out on the bricks. Online resources, such as newsgroups, increase communication, which helps to erase a sense of isolation that dampens self-presentation skills and enthusiasm for new beginnings. In this age of shifting realities, talking to someone else online—someone who is or who has been in jobless shoes—can be an inspiring reminder that it was only your job that ended, not your life.

By the way, the middie mentioned above, who said he was jobless at 50, has a happy ending to his story. Jeff Monson of Dallas has become a successful investment broker.

JOBWEB: A SENSATIONAL NEW RESOURCE TO HELP COLLEGE GRADUATES FIND JOBS

Colleges and universities across the land are grabbing the Internet by the scruff of its neck, and shaking it out on campus to the benefit of America's students.

The Illinois Institute of Technology's career development center operates *1stPlace!,* an online database of students and companies, with a view toward employment. The State of Missouri funds *Project Hire,* a computer network of placement offices of four community colleges, 16 vocational-technical schools, and two comprehensive high schools. The University of Michigan offers online job-hunt assistance to students.

These examples of networking initiatives by institutions of higher education certainly are impressive. But hold onto your gee-whizzes; a new collegiate powerhouse is on the scene.

After two years in blueprints, *JobWeb* is here! The most ambitious career planning and employment effort in the history of American higher education, *JobWeb* is literally revolutionizing the way colleges and universities meet their responsibilities of helping students and graduates find jobs in a changing world.

An A-to-Z virtual employment hub, *JobWeb* was launched last year by the National Association of Colleges and Employers (formerly the College

Placement Council) in Bethlehem, Pennsylvania. *JobWeb's* got it all—from online career research facilities to job placement assistance; from automatic interview scheduling to e-mail and conferencing. Obtain full details from a campus career services office—or watch *JobWeb* on the World Wide Web. Here's a partial list of services now available or in the making:

- ***Help in finding employers***
  By maintaining a comprehensive company directory and database, arranged by industry, geography, and size, *JobWeb* is the new Great Collegiate Muscle Machine for discovering who hires the skills applicants are selling. Employer literature is published on demand. Salary surveys can be viewed at will.

- ***Help in finding employees***
  By operating online job posting services, as well as built-in candidate screening by school, major, and geography, *JobWeb* is a natural assistant to recruiters. Custom job bulletins are available, as well as custom career publications containing employers' information.

- ***"True image" resumes by mail or fax***
  The resumes are sorted by school, major, and region.

- ***A multitude of collateral services***
  Designed to be a comprehensive system, *JobWeb* provides training in Net surfing to campus career counselors, students, and human resource professionals.

To access JobWeb on the World Wide Web:

http://www.jobweb.org

Bear in mind that JobWeb is not restricted to current students and new graduates. Many alumni who have been out of school for years now call their alma maters when they need jobs.

Some college graduates are even checking in at campus career centers of institutions in which they've never set foot before. In these cases, a fee generally is required.

What if you don't live near your old school and can't find a reciprocal agreement at a college nearby? There is always the possibility of long-distance counseling by telephone, but JobWeb's new online collegiate package can give you true interactive access.

THE RISE OF A GLOBAL JOB MARKET

While working on this book, I posted requests, in several newsgroups, for real-life employment stories. The outpouring of e-mail from around the world was exciting. Here's a sliver of the responses.

In England, Thomas F. Lee of Cookham, Berkshire, says he's using the Internet to find freelance jobs as a software consultant and trainer: "My first job came when I answered a newsgroup message which asked if there was anyone available who could train in a type of Windows program. Turns out the chap in question had taken on a bit too much and was looking for help." After that, the work kept on coming over the Net, says Lee.

Georg Fuellen, at one time a German PhD student at MIT, has received five online job offers. His current job, in Germany, resulted from "blindly writing to people whose e-mail address [he] knew from a workshop on biocomputing." His current employer, he says, did require him to send a "CV on paper before he offered me the job."

From Dmitry Rostislavovich Sysoeff comes this e-mail message: "I'm Russian . . . I'm [an] art manager [who found a job online with a German publishing firm] in Moscow. I make telephone and address city book with advertising clips." Sysoeff says he was formerly a programmer in navigation air and sea weapons.

Luca Ciarlatani e-mails me that he's "28 years old and from Italy." He has good credentials: "I'm an electronic engineer with strong experience in both PC hardware and software. . . . I'm a real guru in 3D model managing. . . . I'm looking for a job in the EEC [European Economic Community], U.S., Canada, or Japan." (I don't know the end of Ciarlatani's search; I hope it was happy.)

Herve Schauer contacted this office from Paris, France: "I find all my employees using the Internet, previously using BBS [bulletin board systems]. I used e-mail, as well as posting in the newsgroups. A post only in French in the 'fr.*' hierarchy gives me answers from French-speaking people in countries like Switzerland, Belgium, and Ireland. The Internet is free and very efficient."

From Denmark, Henrik Roseno says: "A Danish weekly newspaper advertised in the newsgroup 'dk.jobs' for an employee who was supposed to work on improving the company's Internet connection. I applied and participated in a job interview."

Kevin Howard reports he's with the Staff Solutions Group in Melbourne, Australia: "We specialise in recruiting for the high tech industry and have recently started to use the Net to source people. We have had some success already."

Database administrator Matteo diTommaso, who moved from Ann Arbor, Michigan, to Hinxton, England last year, found the job online while helping several friends in their job searches by browsing electronic resources. "Without Internet," diTommaso says, "I would never have heard of this opportunity."

As a final illustration, here's a recent message plucked from a mailing list: "The University of Tasmania [Australia] has begun making key resources of the Careers Advisory Service available via the World Wide Web."

The United States has never had a national job market organized like, say, a national stock market. Now, a global job market, centered on the Internet, is growing up around us.

ONCE UPON A TIME THE INTERNET OPENED THE WORLD

You know the Internet is roaring along when you begin to see articles urging social equality in its use—perhaps through freenets, such as the pioneering freenets in Cleveland, Ohio (United States), and in Victoria, British Columbia (Canada).

Questions already are being asked in many quarters about how to avoid a society of information "haves" and "have-nots." Unemployed individuals often are denied access to the Internet because of their inability to purchase the required hardware and their lack of knowledge of how to use it. It's important to address these issues in an era when dramatic restructuring of the world economy has tipped the job market on its ear.

For many people who are jobless, just finding potential employers isn't as easy as it once was. The majority of jobs in manufacturing are no longer in the factories of giant, well-known American companies but in little-known establishments with fewer than 500 people.

Service companies are small and widely scattered. Large numbers of people are telecommuting, or otherwise working from home.

The high-rise downtown office buildings with company names etching the skylines are being replaced by low-rise suburban business parks with moderate signage. In the business park where my office is located, about one-third of the companies lack signs because proprietors don't want people walking in to ask for jobs they can't offer.

Employers have become more cautious about hiring, too, because lawsuits have made it costly to fire nonperformers. Partly for this reason, and partly because of increasing costs of hiring permanent core employees, temporary employment is being used as a way to try out potential employees. The contingency employment trend—now, by some estimates, one third of U.S. jobs—is forcing people everywhere to become far more adept at job hunting than ever before. They have to do it many more times.

All these developments add up to an unescapable fact. In a new and unfamiliar era, job seekers need every available search tool they can lay hands on.

As Megan McLaughlin said in different words, the information age is not right around the corner. It is here today. Once upon a time the Internet opened the world; that time is now.

2 Getting Net Results

The information highway is the exciting new fast track to jobs and employees, business clients, and consulting contracts. Meet some of the people who already are on the roadway, and watch out for employment scams.

JOB FINDER SAYS MOST PEOPLE DON'T KNOW ONLINE JOB HUNTING EXISTS

"The problem for most people is not that using the online system is difficult, but that most people are unaware that online job hunting even exists," says Don Brown, a control engineer in Indianapolis.

Brown, who found his job at Assembly Systems, Inc., by searching through E-Span, a commercial online job listing service headquartered in Indianapolis, is pleased as punch with his electronic experience.

"I searched for a job for two years using traditional methods of job hunting. After only 20 days using online job searching methods, bingo! I got a great job," Brown explains.

The engineer also likes the detail he found online: "In comparison with the traditional methods, the online service I used provides more detailed information. A lot of the jobs online have not been widely advertised, so you are a step ahead of all those who have not yet discovered online job search."

JOB TRAVELERS ON THE INTERNET

Here are seven more true vignettes illustrating the employment experiences of people on the Internet.

Musician Searches for Gigs

Gene Pope owns MusiComp (gpope@sam.neosoft.com), a company located in Houston, Texas. Pope is available for many roles, including trombonist, copyist, arranger, MIDI consultant (computer-composed music), and PC consultant.

Pope finds jobs by browsing through the Internet, looking for contacts and "gigs." When he finds something he likes, he inquires further.

Generally, Pope prefers the jobs advertised online to those he finds in print sources, because more of the online jobs are computer-related.

Pope, who is highly computer-literate, believes that one only needs to be moderately skilled with computers to be able to read about jobs online.

Pope definitely recommends that others look online for jobs. One recruitment ad asked for a Dixieland band; it was very specific. He personally finds most job ads to be on target with the position's requirements.

Pope says he initially discovered online job hunting when he "stumbled across a newsgroup pertaining to employment."

"Through newsgroups in Usenet, it is very easy to find your target audience and the talent pool is much larger than what can be found in traditional ways."

From Army to Civilian Job

Carol Vernon (not her real name) was leaving the Army when she began a job search that ended in employment as a documentation specialist at a major corporation in Minneapolis, Minnesota.

Vernon was using a variety of tools—newspapers, job fairs, military transition assistance, and online search. The online search paid off.

There were potholes along the way: "I was really lucky," Vernon says. "There were a lot of questionable ads online and I had to wade through them to find the more legitimate jobs that interested me."

Bypassing keyword searches (read more about keywords in Chapter 3), Vernon made a general search, using systems that resemble the classified ads in newspapers.

"I ended up answering an ad that asked for former military personnel with technical backgrounds," she says. "I really didn't have the technical background they were looking for, but I took a chance. Fortunately, the company was interested in me."

Vernon says it isn't necessary to be really skilled with computers to search for jobs online.

"I wouldn't suggest that people search exclusively online, but it is one more place to look for jobs. You can also meet people online while networking, and these people might eventually develop into job opportunities," she says.

Vernon encountered lots of junk ads but learned to deal with the flotsam: "At first, it takes a long time to pick through all the ads to find the legitimate ones," she says, "but, as you progress, you start to get a feel for the ones that are legitimate and the ones that aren't."

Holding Out for the Perfect Job

John Blakely became the director of software engineering at Magnet Interactive Studios in Washington, DC, by searching online. Blakely was able to take his time and ended up spending five months in a search for an ideal job.

"I was lucky and could afford to pick and choose because I had time," Blakely admits. "Once I began using the online service, it became much easier for me to find jobs that suited my interests."

"By searching online, you can search by specific fields and geographical locations," says Blakely. "It isn't as tedious as looking through other media because the computer takes care of all the grunt work for you," Blakely explains.

Junk ads? For the most part, Blakely reports, he found better jobs online than elsewhere.

Blakely is now in a position to hire at his company, and he uses the E-Span service. He has recommended the use of online job hunting to many of his friends.

He found out about online job searching by accident. Exploring America Online, Blakely found a job listing database. He began accessing the service through his home computer. After becoming more familiar with search techniques, Blakely began seeking jobs exclusively through the online service.

"Online job hunting definitely gives people an edge," Blakely says. "The online jobs are usually updated more quickly than other media. This makes a big difference because you can find jobs and send out your resume before most people even know there's a job opening."

Blakely feels that, for anyone, online job searching is a great opportunity. "If I had not discovered online job hunting, I might not have the dream job that I have today," he says.

Techie Sees Non-Techies Coming Online

"Most jobs I see posted are of a technical nature, but that is starting to change. Recently, I have seen posts for sales, support, and even some completely unrelated fields—pizza delivery!"

That's the word from Alan Hudson, a systems developer at Insurance Systems Group in Raleigh, North Carolina. He aids in directing the design and development of company IVR (interactive voice response) software.

Before landing this job through online search, Hudson was in the job market for three months. Hudson found out about job hunting online via the Internet at North Carolina State University, his alma mater. "North Carolina State puts out a list of all jobs available at the campus. This includes everything from computer jobs to management to janitorial staff."

Hudson expects that, within a few years, "almost all technical jobs will be online. Other types of jobs will probably be cross-posted to both newspapers and online."

To sum up his attitude toward online job hunting, Hudson states that he has found it to be "the most time-efficient and viable way to search for a job. It is quickly opening jobs that were previously only available through contacts inside a company."

Federal Employee Finds Math Job

Steve McGrath is a mathematician for the Naval Air Warfare Center Weapons Division in China Lake, California. McGrath was never really looking for a job, but signed up with the Federal Research Service, a firm specializing in government information, to try it out.

"Looking through the jobs, I saw a lot of them that I would have applied for had I been looking for a job," McGrath recalls. "The online job search method made it easy to locate jobs in my field."

How tough is it to use the online systems? "You just have to be able to log in," advises McGrath. "If you can do that, then you are pretty much able to use the program."

McGrath has recommended online job searching to others who have been looking for jobs.

"It is a lot easier to search for jobs online than through other methods," says McGrath. "It may be a little more expensive if you stay online for a while, but it is well worth it. It saves a lot of time."

Career Pro Takes Own Advice

Lee W. Waldrep, PhD, completed his doctorate in counseling and development and worked in a one-year temporary position in the career development center at George Mason University in Virginia. He helped seniors search online for jobs; when it was his turn, he practiced what he had preached. In Waldrep's own words:

"In anticipation of my temporary position ending, I began seriously searching electronically in November of 1993; by the summer of 1994, I [had] found a fine position as assistant director of the career development center at the Illinois Institute of Technology in Chicago. IIT is a private research university for science, engineering, and the professions.

"My electronic search included the use of Listservs and the Internet to find out about possible positions, including the one I now hold. Because my prospective employers were universities, I researched their campuses by accessing their campuswide information systems via Gopher." (See Chapter 3 for discussions of these tools.)

Waldrep is a strong advocate of preinterview employer research:

"In one instance, I had a phone interview with limited notice. Because I owned a computer and modem, I was able to access their campuswide information system and learn a great deal about the university in a short amount of time. The first interview probe was, 'Tell us what you know about our university.' This gave me a perfect opening to state what I had learned and share with them how I accessed the information. I think they were impressed with my resourcefulness."

Now that Waldrep is a professional in online search i   ̶
for others:

"Electronic job searching is not just applying for po ̶̶
ads; it is also networking and doing employer research."

Looking Onward and Upward

Henry Feltman (not his real name) has been using the In ̶̶
two years in his search for a new job. He hopes to keep ▬▬
"Don't tell my employer that I'm looking."

Feltman says the Internet is a great way to:

1. Find out what's going on in different geographic ̶̶
2. Find out which skills are hot and which ones are ̶̶
3. Get in touch with recruiters in different areas.

In his words, Feltman's experience in the online job sear ̶̶
been:

a. "Read ad, and e-mail or fax resume.
b. Someone calls for a prescreen [screening out of ̶̶ plicants].
c. Two to three phone interviews, taking about o ̶̶ time.
d. No response. If I call at all, they decide to decli ̶̶ offer) a day or two after the call."

Feltman's online search has produced 15 interviews, b ̶̶
thinks he knows why—he has hit the top of a saturated ▬▬

"The Internet isn't a magic wand," Feltman says. "I ▬▬
hard to move in the familiar job market, they'll be hard to ̶̶
line job market, too."

Feltman's plan: "I've learned things from watching ▬▬
probably go back to school for an MBA (master's in bu ̶̶
tration) or law degree."

INFORMATION HIGHWAY OR HYPE INFORMATI ●▬
KNOW THE DIFFERENCE

Cyberscams ranging from electronic chain letters to pe ̶̶
dles aren't the only bad actors on the Internet.

Federal Employee Finds Math Job

Steve McGrath is a mathematician for the Naval Air Warfare Center Weapons Division in China Lake, California. McGrath was never really looking for a job, but signed up with the Federal Research Service, a firm specializing in government information, to try it out.

"Looking through the jobs, I saw a lot of them that I would have applied for had I been looking for a job," McGrath recalls. "The online job search method made it easy to locate jobs in my field."

How tough is it to use the online systems? "You just have to be able to log in," advises McGrath. "If you can do that, then you are pretty much able to use the program."

McGrath has recommended online job searching to others who have been looking for jobs.

"It is a lot easier to search for jobs online than through other methods," says McGrath. "It may be a little more expensive if you stay online for a while, but it is well worth it. It saves a lot of time."

Career Pro Takes Own Advice

Lee W. Waldrep, PhD, completed his doctorate in counseling and development and worked in a one-year temporary position in the career development center at George Mason University in Virginia. He helped seniors search online for jobs; when it was his turn, he practiced what he had preached. In Waldrep's own words:

"In anticipation of my temporary position ending, I began seriously searching electronically in November of 1993; by the summer of 1994, I [had] found a fine position as assistant director of the career development center at the Illinois Institute of Technology in Chicago. IIT is a private research university for science, engineering, and the professions.

"My electronic search included the use of Listservs and the Internet to find out about possible positions, including the one I now hold. Because my prospective employers were universities, I researched their campuses by accessing their campuswide information systems via Gopher." (See Chapter 3 for discussions of these tools.)

Waldrep is a strong advocate of preinterview employer research:

"In one instance, I had a phone interview with limited notice. Because I owned a computer and modem, I was able to access their campuswide information system and learn a great deal about the university in a short amount of time. The first interview probe was, 'Tell us what you know about our university.' This gave me a perfect opening to state what I had learned and share with them how I accessed the information. I think they were impressed with my resourcefulness."

Now that Waldrep is a professional in online searching, he has a tip for others:

"Electronic job searching is not just applying for positions listed in ads; it is also networking and doing employer research."

Looking Onward and Upward

Henry Feltman (not his real name) has been using the Internet for about two years in his search for a new job. He hopes to keep his quest quiet: "Don't tell my employer that I'm looking."

Feltman says the Internet is a great way to:

1. Find out what's going on in different geographic regions.
2. Find out which skills are hot and which ones are not.
3. Get in touch with recruiters in different areas.

In his words, Feltman's experience in the online job search process has been:

a. "Read ad, and e-mail or fax resume.
b. Someone calls for a prescreen [screening out of unqualified applicants].
c. Two to three phone interviews, taking about one hour in total time.
d. No response. If I call at all, they decide to decline (making a job offer) a day or two after the call."

Feltman's online search has produced 15 interviews, but no offers. He thinks he knows why—he has hit the top of a saturated labor market.

"The Internet isn't a magic wand," Feltman says. "If your skills are hard to move in the familiar job market, they'll be hard to move in the online job market, too."

Feltman's plan: "I've learned things from watching the postings. I'll probably go back to school for an MBA (master's in business administration) or law degree."

INFORMATION HIGHWAY OR HYPE INFORMATION? KNOW THE DIFFERENCE

Cyberscams ranging from electronic chain letters to penny-stock swindles aren't the only bad actors on the Internet.

"Watch out for the junk ads"—this message came from at least a dozen correspondents. Here's a paraphrasing of a typical ad that you should pass by:

WANTED: UPLOADERS

Join the shareware marketing revolution. We need uploaders to upload shareware to sites worldwide. If you are willing to dedicate a couple of hours a day, you can make a serious amount of money, right from your own home computer. The shareware we distribute has a high percentage of registrations, so what this means to you is a lot of commission checks.

Translation: What this really means to you is a commission-only sales job, in which you try to get payment for shareware.

Stay away from so-called international recruiting firms that advertise for such things as "English conversion instructors" to teach in Korea. Lots of college seniors who hope to teach English abroad for a year or two fall for this one. The recruiting firm typically requests that candidates submit a $100 nonrefundable application fee, or a $200 deposit "refundable when they arrive in Korea."

Never pay for a job in advance, even if the money supposedly is for a sample case of the product. One woman e-mailed to me this tale: "I responded to a marketing job after I posted an ad that said, 'Please send info about at-home work for a single mom with two children.' Now I am involved with an electronics firm and have to pay approximately $65 for the job."

Sometimes the ads are outrageous:

If you ABSOLUTELY knew you could make $10,000 a month after two years, would you try a new enterprise? If you ABSOLUTELY knew you could increase your life expectancy by two years, would you use an officially licensed product of the U.S. OLYMPIC COMMITTEE to achieve that goal? . . . There is no selling involved and you don't need to quit your job to make LOTS of money.

Another problem already surfacing is the non-job opening. Apparently, some third-party agencies are posting ads that are O.K., except that they are out of date, or, when contacted, the employer is surprised to learn of a job vacancy.

Just because the Internet is shiny and new doesn't mean it's shiny and honest.

3 Information Highway Trip Tickets

Like the trip tickets you order from auto clubs before a journey, here is what every job seeker must know about the Internet's resources and organizing systems—including points of interest and decent places to stay, plus a lineup of online management tools that keep you on course and propel you to your destination.

"READY... SET... GO!"

ROAD SERVICES TO GET THERE FROM HERE

When automobiles first became available, finding the way to anywhere was an adventure. Before our highways were numbered and marked, tourists depended on detailed, worded directions found in automobile travel guides.

Humorist Bennett Cerf once described what happened after the husband cranked up the old Maxwell or Winton and the wife spread open the auto travel guide on her lap.

Off they went, "jogging left at 31.8 miles with trolley tracks," "turning sharp right at 46.7 miles at statue of Ebeneazer Twuffle," or "avoiding steep-graded macadam turn-off at 58.3 miles." But if they missed one imperative turn somewhere along the road, the travelers would find themselves "at a dead end in Princeton, instead of Mrs. Wimpfheimer's country seat in Asbury Park."

Clueless newbies approaching an online job hunt today may feel kinship with those early auto pioneers—much of the time we fumble about, too.

To avoid rebooting, overshooting, endless dead ends, and general craziness, take a few moments now to study the services and tools that will become your new best friends for an online job search.

If your technologically dyslexic attention should wander, remember this chuckle: On the I-Way, a fool and his modem are soon parted.

HOW TO LOCK OUT COMPUTER ABUSERS

Let's deal with two common concerns about moving around on the Internet. Several people have explained that they're afraid to hit the Internet to look for jobs because they're afraid of crackers (people who break into the computer systems of others) and viruses (programming disruptions that mess up computers).

It's a real worry. Authorities recently uncovered yet another high-profile case of cyberpunks looping and weaving between computer networks and telephone lines to reach 32 computer systems in the United States. Included among the victims was the National Weather Service, which in turn affects the nation's airlines (dangerous weather, no flying).

The crackers allegedly paid for their invasions with more than $1 million of credit-card calls fraudulently charged to people in the United States. How? They smooth-talked Americans into revealing their credit-card numbers by posing as AT&T Corporation security officials.

Where was the cybergang's base of operations? Not the United States, where suspicion first focused, but in Denmark. The Danish government put 35 computer security investigators on the scam at once, and—not surprisingly—found that the crackers were young men between the ages of 17 and 23. There were at least seven of them sporting such I-Way nicknames as "Dixie," "Wedlock," and "Zephyr."

The cybergang didn't limit its attention to the United States. Its attacks were spread across the Internet, detectable in Japan, Brazil, Israel, and Europe.

What was infuriating was that the Danish crackers weren't even original—no touch of genius or of class. They simply copied most of their working information from hacker bulletin boards available on the Internet.

Cybercops keep trying to leap ahead in security technology and to outthink the bad guys. But so far, it has been a cracker's race to lose.

"The cyberpunks are almost always a few steps ahead of the posse," John Perry Barlow has been quoted as saying. Barlow is a cofounder of the Electronic Frontier Foundation, a group concerned with freedoms in cyberspace.

Now that I've gotten your attention with the worst-case scenario, let's take a common-sense look at computerdom.

Computer systems and networks have plenty to worry about from crackers. According to *The Wall Street Journal,* Air Force investigators, using crackers' tools to invade their own systems, have found they are detected in only 3 percent to 5 percent of all cases. But computer systems and networks have system administrators and security cops who worry about outsiders breaking, Goldfinger-like, into Ft. Computer Knox. Let them worry; it's not really your problem.

The chances that a thief will break into a big resume database, steal your resume, and turn it over to your boss are remote.

Assuming you are using your own computer, not one networked to other computers, don't let these concerns keep you out of the new job game—the way to the future. Here's why.

1. The Internet is a point-to-point network. To allow others into your computer, you have to install and run appropriate software. Without your cooperation, it is unlikely that you will fall victim to a cyberpunk trying to steal your income tax records or new book manuscript. If you're a nervous Nellie, do as I do: Turn the computer off every night.

Be sure not to confuse the security of your computer with the security of your messages or your resume. That's a different issue, one that is mentioned later in this chapter.

2. Don't fear that using the Internet will fling open your computer's doors to a killer virus. When I first began Net traveling, I was inordinately worried that Darth Virus would be whooshed into my computer and end it all. "Are you sure . . . are you *really* sure bringing in all this outside stuff isn't going to trash my computer?" I asked my technical associates ad infinitum. Well, so far, so good. No viruses.

Writing in a major reference, *The Internet Unleashed,* anticracker and antiviral expert Billy Barron says, "During my years on the Internet, I have literally downloaded several thousand programs and have never once seen a virus." But Barron cautions that viruses *are* out there; he vaccinates against them and suggests others do the same.

One suggestion: Be as picky about where you get files as you are about where you eat. Well known (file transfer protocol) sites are usually O.K.

Another suggestion: Never fail to use antiviral software on your computer. Most of the recent operating system software has the antiviral protection built in.

For chapter and verse on making your computer a fortress, either read Billy Barron's excellent report, or ask for tips at your favorite computer store.

THE CENTRAL IDEA OF INTERNET JOB SEARCH

Thanks primarily to the advice from author Tracy LaQuey (*The Internet Companion;* see the Appendix), I better understand the framework of Internet services and tools by keeping my compass pointed to a central, defining thought. You may find it useful to remember that same thought:

> **For job hunters, the Internet is a way to**
> 1. **communicate with people, and**
> 2. **find information.**

The first group of services and tools, described in the next section, is intended to help you communicate with people. The second group, later in the chapter, focuses on finding information.

When there is a dual purpose—contacting people *and* finding information—the service or tool is placed in the first group.

THE BASICS OF GETTING CONNECTED

As you become familiar with the groups of services and tools, keep in mind that there are various ways to jump onto the Net. Here are the common ways:

- Through your work; although this access is generally not wise if you're job hunting, it is a marvelous idea if you're hiring with the full knowledge of others in your organization.

NetNote

Importance of Keywords

At the center of job search online or on the Internet is the concept of *keywords*. Most keywords are nouns that describe skills, education, experience, or characteristics.

Some examples of keywords that might show up on a resume are: graphic designer, college graduate, five years' experience, and Dallas resident.

Keywords are also called buzzwords and descriptors. In computerized systems, employers use keywords to search and retrieve from a database; job seekers use keywords to search job ads for those offering the best fit between the job seekers' qualifications and the jobs' requirements.

When searching the Internet resources for employment-related information, try these keywords:

Employment opportunities	Career development
Job listings	Jobs
Jobs offered	Job search
Job postings	Employment on the Net
Job hunting	

- Through a BBS (bulletin board system).
- Through a commercial online information service.
- Through an Internet service provider.

GROUP 1: COMMUNICATING WITH PEOPLE

Bulletin Board Systems

Any computer on a bulletin board system or (BBS) uses a special program that permits other computers to call it over standard telephone lines. Some BBSes are free; others charge an access fee.

Often catering to local communities and special-interest groups, computer bulletin boards are the electronic version of community bulletin boards, like those posted at supermarkets or clubs. They are a way for people to instantly get in touch with one another.

BBSes can be like CB or ham radio, in the sense that individuals can chat with one or more persons by typing messages back and forth. You can use them to send resumes quickly and easily, to ask others for job-opening news, or to check out a locale if you're thinking about relocating.

Job bulletin boards are available in many cities; often they are listed in computer publications. Contract employment services are heavy users of BBSes for job seekers and clients.

Do you run a small business? You can use a BBS for simple e-mail and to distribute information to your staff and customers. A sampling of small businesses using BBSes includes engineering firms, sales organizations, banks, construction companies, travel agencies, and security services.

Bulletin board systems come and go because startup costs can be under $1,000. They are headed by "sysops" (pronounced "siss-opps"), a stand-in for system operators. *Boardwatch,* the BBS industry's leading magazine, says there are more than 60,000 public bulletin boards nationwide. Most of them are run by hobbyists or mom-and-pop entrepreneurs who offer e-mail, file-transfer capabilities, and free or low-cost software programs.

The BBSes have nowhere near the spectrum of resources offered by the national online information services, but they can often provide a cozy electronic meeting place for people with special interests—job seekers, for example, or people interested in a specific career field.

An increasing number of computer bulletin boards are hooked up to the Internet for e-mail. Many BBSes are connected through an informal worldwide network of personal computers called **Fidonet.**

NetNote

New CD-ROM of BBSes

A list of the nation's 60,000 public bulletin boards is being compiled by *Boardwatch* magazine and is expected to be available this year on a CD-ROM disc and as hard copy. Once it is available, focused job seekers can use a keyword search to find all the appropriate BBSes for a particular career field. The price was not available at press time, but will be announced in the magazine. Send e-mail to:

bbs@boardwatch.com

Online information services, such as CompuServe and Prodigy, offer bulletin boards on a wide variety of personal, computing, and professional topics, including jobs and employment.

To reach Fidonet from the Internet, use a domain name (see Glossary) that ends in:

.fidonet.org

You can access Fidonet computers through BBSes. Although relatively few Fidonet bulletin boards are job-specific, a number are occupation-specific—nursing and engineering, for example. Whenever people of similar interests gather, expect job news sooner or later.

Freenets

Freenets are bulletin boards that serve their local communities, providing an electronic town hall where the residents of that city or area can meet, get information, and make announcements. Some freenets also provide Internet access.

For a list of freenets and more details, contact the National Public Telecomputing Network at 216-247-5800, or send e-mail to:

info@nptn.org

Online Information Services

CompuServe, America Online, Prodigy, Delphi, GEnie, ZiffNet, and The Well are examples of various kinds of commercial online information services. Sometimes they're described as the "middlepeople" between you and the Internet.

Of these, CompuServe, America Online, and Prodigy are generally considered the Big Three.

Many, perhaps most, job seekers are now entering the online job search via the commercial online information services. (Until recently, the access typically was to technical users who plugged in through their workplace.) As the magazine *PC Computing* says, "Sometimes the fastest way to get the information you need is to veer off the main thoroughfare [the Internet] and shop the surface streets—online services."

Commercial online services deal in *content*—in megadata. By dialing the service with your computer and modem, you can reach the world's biggest candy store and pick out a sweet selection of goodies from online libraries, newspapers, encyclopedias, bulletin boards, clipping services, department stores, travel agencies, and banking services, to name just a few of the available resources.

Unlike libraries and stores, online services are available 24 hours a day, seven days a week.

Some communications consultants think the online services will change dramatically, becoming more like *pipelines* (that is, access providers to the Internet), rather than the content providers they are today.

Other consultants say they'll be both full-service pipelines and content providers.

Some dissenting consultants argue that, within a couple of years, most of the remaining difficulties of delivering information through the Internet will be wiped away—making cyberspace much cozier. With that change, much of the traditional market for today's online services may shift to the pipeline companies—the Internet service providers.

The only certainty is that the time is ripe to start planning for employment adventure. Think of technology as here today, more tomorrow.

Internet Service Providers

After getting the basics of Internet navigation down, the serious job seeker often wants to plunge into the Internet itself and savor its globe-girding information reach, some of which is not yet available through membership in commercial online information services.

The Net reaches the commercial sector and many branches of the government, as well as scientific and medical research institutions, universities, and the Library of Congress, and is linked by e-mail to many independent bulletin boards.

Getting connected to an Internet service provider and traveling around is a little more intricate than moving on the toll roads of a commercial online service. Fortunately, companies everywhere are springing up to help you get aboard. These companies are called by various names: *Internet service provider, Internet access provider,* and *Internet connectivity provider* are the most familiar monikers.

By any name, growth-minded access establishments are working feverishly to simplify, simplify, simplify. The commercial service you select will probably provide you with a learner's kit or custom software that makes it easier to get started. Some services offer licensed commercial software packages for sale, or include in the deal the best shareware or public domain software.

My testers liked *All in One Internet: The Internet Graphical Software Pak and Tourguide Handbook,* a commercial product published by Wentworth Worldwide Media (see the Appendix). With its cheatsheets, simple screen pictures, and disks, the product is almost like a distance-learning course on how to use the Net.

A review of online search literature released during the past couple of years shows how fast things are moving. (For instance, a guide published in 1993 says modems that work at 2400 baud are perfectly fine; now, they're antiques.)

Within a few years, you'll probably be able to instruct your PC to dial a number, work out a communications arrangement with a far-off host computer, and handle other tiresome details; your job will be to log in, answer a few simple questions, sit back, and let your PC bring home the infobacon.

If the secret of Internet access success is still behind a mental wall, here's how to find the sliding panel to the passageway.

A Ticket to Ride (But in Which Class?)

Review the points of entry from which you reach the Net through an Internet service provider (Chapter 7 takes this topic further):

Dedicated Internet Service—a level of service appropriate for businesses and institutions that need a high-speed, continuous connection to the Internet. Prices vary, but the setup can be costly and the monthly charges can run in the $2,000 range. You can't very well job hunt on your employer's time, but you can ask your company's computer experts to introduce you to the Net.

Almost Dedicated Service (SLIP, PPP accounts—see the Glossary)—a dedicated line that can be timeshared for a specific monthly fee. Many BBSes run a SLIP or PPP connection to the Internet, using a fast modem and a normal telephone line. With that arrangement, they may be considered more as Internet service providers than as BBSes. SLIP and PPP accounts are not easy to set up, but many people find them easy to use.

Comment: The average job hunter will not need a SLIP or PPP account to read e-mail; a dial-up account will do just fine. Now that easier-to-use commercial online services are opening into formerly closed net areas, SLIP and PPP connections may become history for most job hunters' needs.

Morgan Davis, an Internet specialist for CTS Network Services in San Diego (a large Internet service provider), expects the opposite to happen. "We're seeing a trend now where more than 80 percent of our subscribers choose SLIP or PPP, and software is becoming better and better. It may get to the point where the differences between a regular dial-up account and SLIP/PPP are so blurred that people will look back on a dial-up account as an artifact. Microsoft and Apple are both putting [Internet protocol] services into their next operating systems. Going out on the Net with direct access will be as common as using the ATM machine," says Davis.

Dial-Up Service—a shell account (see the Glossary) that lets you dial into the service provider's computer. You may be dialing into a commercial service's own dedicated line, or into a bulletin board operating a SLIP or PPP line. To most people, this is an entirely satisfactory way to get into the Net, but you do have to "double download"—first to the host computer, and then to yours—when pulling in a file.

UUCP (Unix-to-Unix Copy Protocol)—an older, subclass of dial-up access that is, in effect, limited to e-mail and Usenet news. To use it well, you need to be familiar with Unix commands.

Checklist for Choosing an Internet Service Provider

1. Will you receive the exact features, performance, and support you need from the service?

2. Does the service offer full Internet connectivity, including the World Wide Web? The Web is the fastest growing service within the Internet; its relationship to e-mail is about what television is to radio. Or does the service merely offer a gateway to one or two options like e-mail and Gopher?

3. Does the advertised rate cover the service's offerings fully, or is there an extra charge for each additional service? Are you billed by the hour or do you pay a flat monthly fee? (The latter is preferable.)

4. Does the service provide toll-free access?

5. Does the service's staff maintain a savvy customer support crew who will answer any number of questions without losing their calm demeanor?

6. Does the service support a 14,400 bps or faster modem? If so, must you pay more for the faster transmission rate?

E-Mail

Often the fastest and most convenient way to communicate, e-mail is (as the networkMCI Business television commercial said) how Shakespeare would get the word out if he were alive today.

One of the world's richest men, Microsoft CEO Bill Gates, has been using e-mail for years. That should tell you something. Fortune magazine says there are some 28 million electronic mailboxes in the U.S. business community.

If that's not reason enough to hit the e-mail trail, consider the fact that you can communicate via e-mail from the middle of nowhere. Coast Guard Commander Mike Powers and his colleagues, stationed on the USCGC Polar Sea in the Arctic Ocean, did just that. The cutter was part of last year's U.S.-Canadian joint expedition of 70 scientists. They hooked up to the Internet when a satellite was in range to transmit to a Miami computer. Powers says his crew exchanged data with family and colleagues at home, hearing back in a day or two.

Inspired? Start practicing your e-mail skills now—at least a month before you are ready to launch your big job hunt. How? By subscribing to an online information service—currently the dead-cinch way to tap into an e-mail network.

By the way, don't confuse e-mail with fax. A fax is a graphic image that is sent over regular telephone lines by modems, either from a fax machine or from a fax modem in your computer. E-mail over the Internet is text or other data that can be sent over a variety of network links—everything from dial-up to fiber-optic lines. E-mail is usually much cheaper, especially when sent to many people or over long distances.

An important reminder to job hunters: NEVER assume e-mail is secure. The chances that your boss will find out you are job shopping aren't great, but even innocent errors occur—a message might be forwarded through a fluke. Put this caution on any resume that you don't want floating around the Internet:

CONFIDENTIAL. DO NOT FORWARD.

(Chapter 7 covers basic e-mail techniques.)

Mailing Lists

A form of e-mail, mailing lists are a way to send a single message to a group of people.

To subscribe to a mailing list, use e-mail to send a request to the mailing list administrator; include your Internet address. You can cancel a subscription the same way: Send an e-mail message to the list's administrator.

Most (e-mail) listservers—including the popular *Listserv* and the newer *Majordomo*—spit out lots and lots of messages. This can offer strong career management potential if you select the right lists. A couple of college-personnel lists I monitor, for instance, are not designated as job or career lists. Nevertheless, I note that subscribers will from time to time mention job openings they hear about and may go into great detail

---

NetNote

The Group Players

Although terminology varies, here's one way to categorize Net groups you can use to communicate with people:

Discussion Groups is an umbrella term under which the following groups can be arranged:

> —*Mailing lists*
> > Including listservers (such as *Listserv* and *Majordomo*)
>
> —*Usenet newsgroups*

Mailing lists are e-mail; like magazines, they come to you automatically once you subscribe. By contrast, newsgroups are like going to a movie theater to see a particular film: You must seek out a newsgroup each time you wish to visit it.

---

in the job descriptions. Other subscribers announce their resignations, which may mean their old jobs are up for grabs.

Mailing lists that use *mailbots* are becoming very popular with large and small businesses. A mailbot is an e-mail address that automatically returns your marketing message to potential customers who have initiated an inquiry.

Usenet News

Usenet, a collection of thousands of discussion groups (newsgroups), has been called the heart and soul of the Internet. People use Usenet for many different reasons, but the common denominator is the need to exchange information. Newsgroups are arranged by subject matter and cover just about every conceivable topic, from rocket science to low-cal cooking.

The newsgroups are organized into hierarchies such as science (sci), recreation (rec), society (soc), and jobs (misc.jobs). See Chapter 4 for a more complete discussion of newsgroup hierarchies.

What's on the Internet by Eric Gagnon (see the Appendix) is a delightful book that, while not job-specific, presents Internet resources with sparkling graphics. (Many other books are straight text.)

Gagnon notes a discussion list for dog lovers. Suppose you were a new veterinarian; you could go online and, after you got a feel for the group, decide whether to ask for advice from list subscribers about what part of the country might need a vet. Dog lovers know of vets who may be retiring or in need of a junior colleague.

Usenet is an ideal resource for job shoppers and employers.

GROUP 2: FINDING INFORMATION

Anonymous FTP

File transfer protocol (ftp) is a way to send and receive files. In case you've forgotten, a file can be anything—a report you created in your PC's word processor, plain text, a spreadsheet, a software program— even a picture or music.

Ftp sites are computers where files are kept. Ftp is used both as a noun and a verb in Netspeak. The word "anonymous" is the login name you use, followed by your e-mail address as the password.

Anonymous ftp sites, like the Library of Congress, offer data anybody can have. There are no fees and no special passwords, but keep these two tips in mind:

1. Unlike host computer and e-mail addresses, file names on many ftp archive systems are case-sensitive; you must type in the file and directory name *exactly* as you see them listed.
2. You have to know a site's exact Internet address before you can ftp to it. Files known as *readme* (this is an information file that means what it says: "read me") files may be available to explain what available at the site.

There are other ftp tricks you should know. Books like *The Internet Directory* by Eric Braun (see the Appendix) give you chapter and verse on the anonymous ftp process.

Braun also explains the other big question: Where are all these anonymous ftp archives? They're everywhere—from the National Institutes of Health in Maryland to the University of California at Berkeley, and from Oxford University in England to the National Library of Scotland.

The data you can pull out of an ftp archive seem to be infinite. As Braun says, "Most anonymous ftp archives exist purely by the goodwill of their hosting institutions. Usually they are maintained by volunteers and are run on computers that are used for 'realwork.'"

Braun suggests you begin your search with Archie. Archie who?

Archie

Archie (from the word *archive*) is a computer program—and a very good tracker. The Archie program helps you search anonymous ftp sites around the globe to locate a specific file. You give Archie a file name—or enter a search string.

(A search string is a feature that allows you to search for files by entering a word, phrase, numbers or symbols that may be in the file's title.)

Because the Archie program maintains a database of file information collected from anonymous ftp sites all over the world, and gives you the tools to efficiently search this database, you won't spend untold hours looking in the wrong places. Each ftp site is visited every 30 days, which means the Archie database is relatively current. How do you find Archie? You can use Telnet (see below) to connect to any one of several Archie servers (computers).

Gopher

Using Gopher is like going into a swanky shop, pointing at whatever merchandise you'd like, and saying, "I'll take that . . . and that . . . and that."

Gopher allows you to browse the Gopher-based resources of the Internet. Resources are presented on menus. You don't need to know addresses or special commands. You just highlight an area of interest, select it, sit back, and wait for the item to fill your screen.

If you get lost in Gopher, type the letter "u" (for "up") repeatedly—it will bring you back to the main menu. When you're ready to leave Gopher, type "q" (for "quit").

Want to have a go at some of the more than 5,000 Gopher servers on the Net? Ask your Internet service provider if a local Gopher server is available, which will be the easiest way to "gopher it."

Or, tap into one of the public Gophers at the University of Minnesota, where it was born:

    telnet consultant.micro.umn.edu

Gopher Jewels

Gopher Jewels, one of the better efforts to organize and catalog the Gophers, was started in 1993 to find interesting sites in Gopher-space. Gopher Jewels now points to more than 2,000 gopher sites around the world, organizing them into approximately 100 subject areas. All can be searched by keywords. Most of the sites are in the United States, but overseas sites are blooming constantly.

At press time, the subject index of Gopher Jewels (plus a brief listing of each subject's contents) looked like this:

1. **Gopher Jewels Information and Help**
    Includes Help menus and archived documents.

2. **Community, Global, and Environmental**
    Freenets, Gophers elsewhere, and environmental issues.

3. **Education, Social Sciences, Arts & Humanities**
    Anthropology and archaeology, arts and humanities, education through high school, geography, history, language, religion and philosophy, and social sciences.

4. **Economics, Business, and Store Fronts**
    Products, services, business, and retailing.

5. **Engineering and Industrial Applications**
    Architecture, engineering, and manufacturing.

6. **Government**
    Federal, state, military, and political.

7. **Health, Medical, and Disability**
    Disability, medicine-related, and psychology.

8. **Internet and Computer-Related Resources**
    A list of Gophers with computer- and cyberspace-related subject trees, and Internet resources by type.

9. **Law**
    Legal or law related, and patents and copyrights.

10. **Library, Reference, and News**
    Books, journals, magazines, newsletters, publications, radio and television, and libraries.

11. **Miscellaneous Items**

12. **Natural Sciences, Mathematics**
    Agriculture and forestry, astronomy, biological sciences, chemistry, geology, oceanography, mathematics, meteorology, and physics.

13. **Personal Development and Recreation**
    Employment opportunities and resume postings, fun stuff and multimedia, museums and exhibits, travel information.

14. **Research, Technology Transfer, and Grants Opportunities**
    Technical reports, technology transfer, and grant information.

Many paths exist to Gopher Jewels; here's how to travel to the home of the Jewels.

Gopher to:

    cwis.usc.edu

Veronica

Veronica is a fanciful acronym for *Very Easy Rodent-Oriented Net Index to Computerized Archives.* The rodent reference probably relates to Gopher, a rodent. Veronica's database contains directories and file names that it finds in Gopherspace.

Why was Veronica invented? The first Gopher server started running in 1992. Now, thousands of Gopher sites hang out on Internet-connected computers all over the world. Because there are so many Gopher items, you may go squirrelly trying to find what you want.

Enter Veronica, which allows you to search directory titles and file names with ease. You use keywords to find specific items in the Gopher system.

If, for instance, you searched for the keyword *MBA,* you would get a tailored-for-you menu of directories with that keyword in its labels. You would also get access to the files in those directories, which may or may not have the word *MBA* in their names, but are about subjects relating to those who hold master of business administration degrees.

When you get your menu, you look it over, decide which source you want to look at, and select the item. Veronica will connect you to the Gopher server that stocks that item.

Jughead

The amusing name Jughead stands for *Jonzy's Universal Gopher Hierarchy Excavation And Display.* It is a 1993 utility program serving as a local (not the entire Internet) search feature in Gopher. By using Jughead, you can search all Gopher menus (not the text files themselves) for target keywords in titles.

Jughead is especially helpful when Veronica servers are too busy to help you, or when you want to save time and search only a small area of Gopherspace. For example, if you only want to search the Gopher servers within a particular university or on a specific public access Gopher, Jughead is made to order.

In a retailing analogy, Veronica is a department store and Jughead is a boutique.

You access Jughead the same way you access Veronica—by selecting an item on a Gopher menu.

At the University of Texas at Austin's Gopherspace, here's what Jughead looks like:

Jughead: Search menus in University of Texas at Austin
gopherspace<?>

There are relatively few Veronica servers, but there are a zillion Jugheads, each offering a service for a defined piece of Gopherspace.

In case you're wondering about the names of Archie, Veronica, and Jughead, they are all characters in *Archie* comic books.

Telnet

In the finding-information department, Telnet is the catapult that gets you airborne. This program allows you to electronically zip all over the world and grab files from computers nearby or far away.

The action is called "remote login": You can log into a computer somewhere else if it's open to the public—or if you have permission.

Suppose you secured a job interview for a marketing position with a major distributor of pineapples. You are confident of your job skills, but you're switching industries and you don't know much about pineapples. You could telnet to a computer in a state that grows a lot of the fruit—say, Hawaii—and check its university or library database for news of the pineapple market.

NetNote

Clients and Servers

The words *clients* and *servers* appear frequently in Net lit. Clients are programs that request information for you; servers are computers (or computer networks) that give the information to the clients.

You can use the Gopher client program on your Internet host (where you're hooked up). If your host happens to be fresh out of Gopher clients, you can telnet to one of the many public access Gopher clients available to anyone on the Internet.

If that doesn't produce enough information, you could try a commercial online service, such as DIALOG and its NEXIS news database.

Several programs allow you to browse through the myriad of fabulous resources on the Internet; you can telnet to two of these, the World Wide Web and Gopher. You can also telnet to Archie and WAIS.

The ability to use the Telnet protocol is what really opens vistas to the world's information, and sometimes to its people.

Need career management resources quickly? On your Telnet command, those resources will cross continents and oceans, turning up on your desk when you need them most.

Before you can telnet, you must know where you're going and have an exact Internet address for the destination.

Wide Area Information Servers (WAIS)

Archie tells you *where a file is.* But if you are trying to find a file based on *what's in the file,* one of Archie's cousin systems will do the job.

Welcome to Wide Area Information Servers (WAIS, pronounced "ways").

WAIS searches the Internet by using keywords and phrases that index the contents of documents rather than document titles. Using WAIS is like looking at an index at the back of a book (as compared to a library card catalog which lists book titles only).

WAIS is not as big as Archie or Veronica, but *it can be powerful when you are preparing for an interview in a particular industry or searching the Internet for job listings of a particular type.*

The trouble is, WAIS is no day at the beach. You'll need to read up on it, particularly if you log in through public Internet servers.

A common way to access WAIS indexes is through Gopher (discussed earlier), although the World Wide Web, the topic of the next section, now also provides access. For example, an easy way to use the WAIS tool is to access it through CareerMosaic (see Chapter 4).

How to Use the Internet, by Mark Butler (see the Appendix), a book with lots of helpful pictures and white space, is very good on the mechanics of using WAIS.

World Wide Web

Known by a variety of aliases of its name—*World Wide Web, WorldWideWeb,* the *Web, WWW,* or *W3*—this spectacular Internet tool was born in 1991 and took off in 1993, due in large part to the release of *Mosaic,* a popular *browser, the term for software used to navigate the Web.*

Mosaic is available for free to anyone. It presents information in the point-and-click format that Macintosh and Windows (an IBM-compatible PC operating program) users know so well. Mosaic was developed with public funds at the National Center for Supercomputing Applications at the University of Illinois.

After the initial oohs and ahs over Mosaic subsided, it became apparent that Mosaic works great with a muscle computer and fast modem, but is slow with more modest equipment. This recognition brought a more demanding attitude toward Web browser software writers: *"What have you done for me lately?"*

Within a year of Mosaic's release, a number of commercial software publishers rushed to market with improved versions of the original—or new products entirely.

Netscape Communications Corporation in Mountain View, California, offers *Netscape,* a product that, for many who browse the Internet, is rapidly replacing Mosaic. Other popular new software for Net browsing includes *NetCruiser,* an all-inclusive Internet interface by Netcom On-Line Communications Services, Inc., in San Jose, California; and *Enhanced NCSA Mosaic,* by Spyglass, Inc., in Savoy, Illinois.

Lynx is an older Web browser showing only text (no graphics). Even though Lynx is not flashy, it is fast (you don't have to wait for the graphics to materialize) and that's why a lot of people, especially business-people, still like it.

A new and inexpensive shareware product is a program called *Slip-Knot.* Its claim to fame is a major technological breakthrough. Until Slip-Knot arrived, the ordinary PC user with only a modem and indirect dial-up access could get text, but nothing else, on the WWW.

Now, with the relatively modest access of a modem and dial-up account, SlipKnot can get the whole works—text, pictures, and, if you have a sound card in your computer, sound.

Before SlipKnot debuted, sound and graphic presentations were available only if you managed direct Internet access through SLIP or PPP, or TCP/IP connectivity (see the Glossary for these terms).

SlipKnot is, as people used to say, "for the man or woman on the street," and it, and its successor software, will invite millions more people to the Web's vibrant new culture.

You use SlipKnot with Microsoft Windows when you have a common type of account known as a Unix shell account with your Internet service provider.

Another new product in this category is *The Internet Adapter (TIA)* by Cyberspace Development, Inc. In essence, it converts a shell account into a "pseudo-SLIP" account in the same way that an electrical adapter converts a two-prong outlet into a three-prong outlet. In effect, TIA creates a SLIP account from your shell account, permitting you to run any

Web navigating software, including, for example, Mosaic and Netscape. You can also run popular e-mail software, such as Eudora. TIA is not shareware, but it sells for only $25.

What's the difference between SlipKnot and TIA? SlipKnot is a browser and you must use its interface; TIA is a utility software that allows you to use a variety of interfaces. Pick your favorite.

Most commercial online information services include Web browsers in their Internet connections. New computer operating systems will probably have tools for Web access. The World Wide Web is becoming less tangled every day. In function, the Web resembles one of those encyclopedias on CD-ROM in which you can follow a subject in text, music, pictures, and movies as it branches, and branches again into the distance.

In that sense, the WWW has corralled an infinitely rich collection of existing cyberspace resources and linked them in a hypermedia system. The WWW is to standard Net resource collections as a fancy dress ball is to a block party.

When you fire up Mosaic, you see a screen that looks like a *USA Today* newspaper page with lots of graphic elements. Within those graphic elements are hidden links to other locations on the Internet. Some of the words on the screen are highlighted in a color of your choice, such as blue. When you click on blue words, the program (changing to another color highlight, such as red) leaps to another treasure trove of information somewhere on the Internet—no matter where it is, your hometown or halfway around the world—and displays it on your screen.

Click on the words "Interactive Employment Network\E-Span" and *whoosh!,* you're in Indiana, where E-Span operates a job service listing current job openings. Click on "CareerMosaic," and *whoosh!,* you're in California reading colorful screens of information about major employers.

By following the links, you can leapfrog to related information anywhere on the Web. The Web is growing wings, but at this state of its technology, you'll need patience.

Even with faster browsers, downloading multimedia over a dial-up connection (rather than a dedicated Internet service) isn't fast enough for people who like to get things done in a hurry.

I asked my technical consultant, Steve Eisenberg, how he got so smart. Steve said every time he waits for a [graphical] download from WWW, he reads.

If you'd like to see me on the Web, tune into my publisher's Internet promotion. Here's the case-sensitive address:

http://marketplace.com/0/obs/books/Kennedy/JLKennedy.html

To download a free copy of Mosaic, use the file transfer protocol. Ftp to the National Center for Supercomputing Applications one of the following messages:

ftp for Windows:

ftp.ncsa.uiuc.edu

Type:

cd /Mosaic/Windows
Get readme.now

Follow readme.now instructions

ftp for Macintosh:

ftp.ncsa.uiuc.edu

Type:

cd /Mosaic/Mac
Get QuickStart.Txt

Follow QuickStart.Txt instructions

To download SlipKnot, send a blank e-mail message (no subject, no text) to:

slipknot@micromind.com

To find out more about TIA, call SoftAware Co. (310-314-1466), or Gopher to:

marketplace.com

For other products, contact vendors:

Netscape Communications Corporation: 800-638-7483
Netcom On-line Communications Services, Inc.:800-353-6600
Spyglass, Inc.: 800-647-2201

LOOK OUT, JOBS AHEAD!

We stand on one of history's great dividing lines. This line created by new technology is like those that separated the era of stagecoaches from the heyday of the railroads, and the age of the railroads from the jet age. New jobs and fresh ways of doing business are mere keystrokes and clicks away.

If you're thinking, "This keystroking and clicking stuff sounds great, but how do I get to square one and what buttons do I push once I'm there?," you can turn immediately to the start-up tips in Chapters 7 and 8. Or, you can turn the page and head straight to the focus of this book: jobs.

4 JOBS Looking for People

Here's what you've been waiting for—the places where employers post jobs. From commercial job banks to informal, chatty groups. From corporate America to the U.S. government. The Internet's a splendid source for finding the job you've always wanted.

"OK, SO IT WAS A BAD IDEA TO INSTALL A SIREN THAT GOES OFF EVERY TIME A NEW JOB IS POSTED IN A JOB BANK. DO YOU HAVE A HAMMER?"

ONLINE LIBRARIAN ADVISES FORTUNE 500 COMPANY ON NEW STYLE HIRING

Before trying something new in hiring, corporate America usually seeks guidance from human resource professionals or executive recruiters. One famous West Coast company turned to a librarian on the East Coast.

Margaret F. Riley is the circulation and computer resources librarian at Worcester Polytechnic Institute's Gordon Library in Worcester, Massachusetts. To those of us who tool around on the Net, Riley wears another hat: respected Net pioneer who, early on, figured out that cyberspace is a nice place for job hunters.

To underscore the newness of job cyberhunting, it was only last year that Riley started to become well known for her work in aiding job seekers through the online distribution of a free report she compiles, *Employment Opportunities and Job Resources on the Internet*.

That point was emphasized when one of her employees at the library came to her in the summer and asked if Riley would speak to the employee's husband about hiring on the Internet.

"When I picked up the phone and said, 'Hi,' I was startled to discover I was conference-calling a local management meeting for one of the nation's largest companies 3,000 miles away," Riley recalls.

"We discussed why they should join the Internet, how e-mail can be used to contact colleagues, researchers, and customers, as well as put advertising on the Net through a public server using *Gopher,* or the *World Wide Web*. We discussed how they could recruit new employees through reading *newsgroups* or subscribing to a service that collects resumes, such as the *Online Career Center*," the online librarian says.

Riley says she forgot about the conference call until recently, when her employee came into her office with news. "She told me that her husband had hired a new employee by reading resumes collected from the Internet, selecting a few applicants for interviews, and that he had offered the job to one of the applicants," Riley says.

Actually, it's understandable why the major league company called Riley for a tutorial. Locating resources is a challenge, and deciding how to organize them is an even bigger challenge.

In traditional job guides, it is typical to cluster job services and resources by what they are, *not* how you get to them. You are directed to check with employment agencies, campus career centers, and employers, for example. No one organizes the resources by a transportation system—how you get to them—such as, "services you can reach by car," or "services you can reach by bus."

The needs are different, however, in job cybersearch. For one thing, few people (including me) have in-depth experience with most of these services. For the most part, they're too new to have established a track record. But perhaps more important is the point Riley makes in organizing her list by how you get to the service or resource—how you access it.

"When you cluster by access method, you can search methodically, running the same computer program until you are finished, before switching to another program. It's a more efficient use of the searcher's time," she says.

After reflecting on the organization of this chapter, I couldn't think of a reason *not* to do it Riley's way. With some exceptions, this chapter is organized to somewhat match Riley's *Employment Opportunities and Job Resources on the Internet,* which is updated periodically and made available online without charge.

To access the Riley report by Gopher:

una.hh.lib.umich.edu

Select:

inetdirs
All Guides
Employment Opportunities & Job Resources

To access by World Wide Web:

http://www.wpi.edu/~mfriley/jobguide.html

JOBS YOU REACH VIA COMMERCIAL ONLINE SERVICES

Most of the new computers being delivered today come loaded with software for logging into commercial online services.

That's a fortuitous development because the commercial online services are going gangbusters with lots of job hunting and career planning resources you can pull in with your computer.

If you're an Internet virgin and are clumsy besides, subscribing to a commercial online information service or two is probably your square one move into online job hunting.

The reason: Commercial onlines have a stake in making their wares uncomplicated for you to sample and use.

Which ones are the simplest to deal with? At this writing, most comparisons give the easy-to-use award to America Online, with CompuServe getting a pat on the back for its depth of content.

Within a year, it probably won't matter which ones you try; they're all getting easier.

NetNote

When Addresses Don't Work

When you are employing Telnet, ftp, Gopher, or World Wide Web, you must remember which type of system you're on.

- When you are using a menu-based system (very common when you subscribe to an Internet service provider), you do not have to type the terms "telnet," "ftp, "Gopher" or "www" in front of the Internet address.

- When you are using a Unix shell system (very common at universities and big companies), at the Unix prompt (such as "1%" or "2%"), you do have to type "telnet" followed by a space and then the Internet address; or "ftp" followed by a space and then the Internet address; or "gopher" followed by a space and then the Internet address; or "www" followed by a space and then the Internet address.

- When you are already in a Unix-based program—say, in the Telnet program—you will have to use other Unix commands, such as "open" followed by a space and then the Internet address, to connect to the target resource.

In this book, the Telnet, ftp, Gopher, and WWW addresses are given for a menu-based system.

When you can't get through to a particular resource, four possibilities are common:

1. You have incorrectly typed the address.
2. You are using the wrong commands for your system, as explained above.
3. The address is incorrect—or has changed. Look in another book, or see if you can find it online by using Veronica, Webcrawler, or another search tool described in most basic Internet guidebooks. Or call somebody.
4. The resource is "down" or "under construction." Try again in a day or so.

Computer and online magazines, such as *PC Computing*, regularly do comparative analyses of the commercial onlines. Changes show up every three or four months.

As you may have guessed, most of the commercial onlines have job postings.

In addition, most have other job-related resources as well. Accessing tips are not given because each service gives you navigational guidance when you sign up. Here's a brief look at the commercial onlines.

► **America Online**
800-227-6364

With more than 1.5 million members, AOL is one of the industry's most aggressive onlines. It has a wide range of career-related features, created chiefly by James C. Gonyea. Gonyea also operates *Help Wanted-USA,* through Gonyea and Associates, Inc., 1151 Maravista Drive, New Port Richey, Florida 34655; 813-372-1333.

Help Wanted-USA is a large online database of help-wanted ads. The ads are collected and distributed electronically by independent contractor Gonyea and Associates, Inc. Using a team of more than 60 employment consultants across the nation, more than 6,000 ads are online each week through America Online and the Internet.

Another service of Gonyea and Associates is the *Worldwide Resume/ Talent Bank.* It enables job seekers to post their full resume electronically through America Online and the Internet.

Gonyea created and directs America Online's Career Center, which offers an enormous range of services, including counseling, an employer contacts database, listings of executive search firms, occupational profiles, and resume guides.

In addition to the Career Center, AOL offers a wide variety of online places where subscribers can meet, get advice, and discuss career-related issues. These areas include *People's Connection* ("real-time" chatting), and interest groups for lawyers, educators, aviation specialists, and veterinarians.

Other special interest groups include: Health Professionals Network, Nurses Network, Writer's Club, SeniorNet (part-time work for seniors), National Professional Photography Association, BikeNet (jobs available message board), and National Public Radio Online (educators' network). *The Exchange Message Boards* are opportunities to network and gain information on dozens of careers and career-related topics.

Also available on America Online is *Hoover's Handbook,* a guide featuring detailed analyses of 500 of the nation's largest corporations.

AOL has an exciting new venture, the Internet Services Company, which will make it very easy to use lots of the Internet universe, including the World Wide Web.

► **CompuServe**
800-848-8199

CompuServe, a giant subsidiary of H&R Block, Inc., has more than 3 million subscribers and a huge database of information. Most subscribers are professional and business accounts—just what you, the job hunter or employer, want. The largest concentration of subscribers is in the United States, but CompuServe members are found in 150 other nations.

NetNote

Case Sensitivity: A Capital Idea or Lower Case

In a time long ago, when keypunch machines and terminals only had capital letters, EVERYTHING WAS WRITTEN IN UPPER CASE. IT WAS A REAL PAIN TO READ.

Later, keypunches went to museums and terminals learned to read lower case. Thus, computers switched to the mixed case of normal writing.

Then some computers—mainly those running Unix programming—gave uppercase and lowercase terms different meanings, even though most computers treat the cases in an identical manner.

To explain: On a Unix system, FILE.ABC, File.ABC, and file.abc are three different files, but most other systems accept them as just three different ways to name the same file. Sometimes, the case sensitivity issue can gum up an e-mail address. Usually, case doesn't matter in the domain part of the address (the part after the @) sign. But the local part (the part before the @ sign) can vary.

Directory names and file names never include spaces. Computers seek file names by reading strings of letters, numbers, and punctuation marks with no spaces in them.

A rule of thumb follows. It is not perfect, but it will do most of the time. When you are maddeningly thwarted in your Internet pursuits, and are wondering which stooge you are, the first thing to check is case sensitivity.

- Most communications should be lowercase, including names of people, e.g.:

    michael@ace.org.

- Names of files you are transferring (ftp) should be written in exactly the same upper- and lowercase mix that appears in a directory listing, e.g.:

    README.ftp.

The service is flush with attractions for job seekers. The *Journalism Forum* serves the professional with job listings, libraries, freelance opportunities, and ideas.

The *Executive News Service* allows CompuServe members to customize their incoming news clips and gives them up-to-the-minute news about companies in which they are professionally interested. The *Business*

Database Plus feature provides access to magazine articles in business publications. It's searchable by keywords and useful to job seekers interested in learning more about different companies.

The *Disclosure* database is compiled from the 10Ks and other reports that all publicly owned companies file with the Securities and Exchange Commission—a superb source of career management research.

Want a listing for 9.2 million businesses in the United States and 1.6 million in Canada? All businesses listed in the 5,300 Yellow Page directories in the two countries are included in *Biz*File* on CompuServe.

Of CompuServe's 700-plus forums, in excess of 200 are professional forums offering splendid opportunities to interact with people in various career areas.

▶ Delphi
800-695-4005

Owned by Rupert Murdoch and linked to Murdoch's News Corporation, Delphi Internet Services Corporation is growing by leaps and bounds. Career seekers, take notice.

Let's start with the entertainment business. One of Delphi's new focuses is entertainment, and now subscribers can talk directly with film and TV producers, celebrities, magazine editors, and authors.

That's only the beginning. Delphi Internet offers members lots more resources for finding a job. *The Business Forum* features classified ads that list job and business opportunities and tips on conducting business and public relations activities.

Delphi Internet also offers discussion groups, called Custom Forums, that provide professionals with a wide spectrum of career information. *The Job Complex* gives up-to-the-minute information on job offerings, business ventures, resumes, employee and employer rights, job benefits, at-home businesses, and career consultations. This forum is a valuable resource, whether you are beginning your career search, or are interested in continuing education for your occupation.

The Nursing Network forum allows nurses, or those who are interested in becoming nurses, to learn about job openings and educational developments, reference materials, and accredited independent study offerings.

The Self-Employment forum provides an attractive place for people to learn—directly from those who have done it—how to start, operate, and thrive in a one-person or small business.

No doubt about it, Delphi's custom forums offer subscribers the opportunity to interact and exchange ideas with professionals in a wide range of career fields.

▶ GEnie
800-638-9636

GEnie, a General Electric company, has lots of career and small business places to go. The *Home Office/Small Business RoundTable* is a discussion group that brings rave reviews. The *Writers RoundTable* is an electronic association of writers; members give tips to improve writing skills, and advice on getting published. Other RoundTables focus on medicine, law, education, law enforcement, military service, aviation, romance writers, and desktop publishing.

Interested in an international job? GEnie's got RoundTables for many nations in Europe, plus Japan and Canada.

A photographer's marketing list is available for freelance shutterbugs. The *Dr. Job* feature helps with career problems.

With dozens of professional RoundTables, GEnie is a valuable resource for tracking down business opportunities, for job hunting, and for day-to-day networking.

▶ **Prodigy**
800-776-3449

Once you get to the Menu of Career Opportunities on Prodigy, one of the largest commercial online services (more than 2 million subscribers), you can choose *Careers BB* (a bulletin board), *Classifieds* (job listings), or several other kindred services.

Under the list of topics on Careers BB, you'll find these options:

Career change, position wanted, relocating, accounting, airline, arts & entertainment, civil service, communications, computer, consulting and court reporting.

You'll also discover topics for design and construction, engineering, entrepreneurs, financial, fire and emergency medical service, insurance, legal, management, medical and veterinary, military, nursing, police, sales and retailing, travel, secretarial, and union trades.

Within these topics are many more subjects.

There's a local angle, too. Prodigy, in conjunction with a number of newspapers, offers segmented databases, information on location communities, local bulletin boards, newspaper content, including classified ads, and more. The emphasis is *local*. If you don't want to relocate for a job, the Prodigy/newspaper tie-ins are a natural.

Among newspapers teaming up with Prodigy are the *Atlanta Journal-Constitution, Los Angeles Times, Milwaukee Journal, Milwaukee Sentinel, New York Newsday, and Tampa Tribune*. As part of its company research, note that Prodigy offers, through the Dow Jones Company News, 21 days' worth of past and present articles on publicly traded companies.

AstraNet is a new, independent Prodigy service—with a spectacular web browser—that offers content to a variety of Internet market segments on the World Wide Web. Launched in late 1994, AstraNet is expanding in stages. First offerings are in sports, finance, news, and government. AstraNet has a mix of for-free and for-fee services. You can take a peek at AstraNet on the Web.

To access by World Wide Web:

http://www.astranet.com

OTHER COMMERCIAL ONLINE SERVICES

The relentless risc in online interest has fueled expansion of many regional commercial online services—and given birth to several new, potentially major players.

The Well (415-332-4335) in the San Francisco area is famous for its computer smarties, hipsters, and other interesting subscribers. **Echo (212-255-3839)** is a trendy New York electronic salon that attracts many women. **Transom (800-475-9689)** calls to the 18- to 34-year-old market. Apple Computer's **eWorld (800-775-4556)** is still spicing its recipe for cybersuccess. **Interchange (800-595-8555)** is Ziff-Davis's new online service.

The biggest new kid on the virtual block is turning out to be Microsoft's online service, the **Microsoft Network.** It is a significant force in the online market because it's bundled with the company's new Microsoft Windows 95 operating software. That is, in addition to the Windows 95 software that many computer users will buy to upgrade existing operating software, millions of new computers will come equipped with Windows 95, which has built-in online access to the Microsoft Network.

The Microsoft Network will act as a platform for independent providers of content and services, who will offer their own pricing options.

The number of commercial online subscribers topped 5 million at the end of 1993, up from 1.2 million in 1989, according to Simba Information, a market researcher in Wilmington, Connecticut. In 1996, that number is expected to be vastly larger. The typical individual subscribes to more than one service.

As prices fall, online navigation becomes easier, and graphics explode in a riot of color, it's a safe bet that millions more subscribers will soon be buying tickets to the commercial online celebration.

BEST NET BETS: JOB POSTINGS

Until now, the jobs posted on the I-Way have tended to be focused on computer, electronics, and engineering careers. The new assortment includes many more sales, marketing, health, and other less technically oriented positions, as well as a ballooning number of entry-level jobs.

Because the online employment industry is being created as you read this book, some of the resources described in the sections that follow may fade quickly, as others debut. When we went to press early this year, the resources listed received a third and final verification by a team of computer-wise checkers, and are thought to be accurate.

Most of the BBSes are free to job seekers. But you should consider paying to subscribe to an especially valuable bulletin board.

On the topic of payment, before using a resource cited in this book, always check whether it is for-free or for-fee. Every effort has been made to accurately indicate which resources are going to cost job seekers and which are not, but things change. A BBS labeled "commercial," for example, may be free to job seekers but cost employers; or it may cost both parties. If you must give a credit card number to participate, that's a clear sign you're going to be charged a fee.

JOBS YOU REACH THROUGH BULLETIN BOARD MODEMS

Job-listing bulletin boards—computer message boards with a list of job openings—are not easily pigeonholed because their job inventories often overlap. For this book, they are divided into three broad groups:

1. **Private sector jobs**—all occupations, including technical and nontechnical, entry-level and advanced-level positions; some government jobs are included, but the bulk of the jobs are in the private sector. In several instances, the jobs are chiefly in the private sector, although the BBS is operated by a public agency. At first glance, it looks weird, but remember, the public employment service has private sector jobs in its job banks.
2. **Technical jobs**—only technical jobs.
3. **Government jobs**—only federal, state, and local jobs.

At the end of most of the listings in this section, the modem telephone number appears in boldface type. Generally, your communications software (such as Procomm Plus, or Qmodem Pro) should be set to the following parameters:

No Parity, 8 databits, 1 stopbit, Full Duplex, and either **ANSI terminal emulation,** or **VT 100 terminal emulation.**
N,8,1,F, ANSI
    or
N,8,1,F, VT 100

NetNote

Some BBSes Are Free but Could Use a Few Appreciation Dollars

Most of the free bulletin boards are kept going by volunteers using their own funds. If you find a board to be helpful, send the sysop $5 or so to defray costs of telephone lines, replace computer parts, and so forth. Some of the sysops tell me they'll have to shut down their boards if they don't get relief in the form of a few bucks now and then. We're not talking big money, just a little appreciation.

As one sysop told me, "My wife says, 'Don't even think about buying a new hard drive to upgrade your bulletin board. We've been married four years and we don't have a dining room table yet.'" See what I mean? Be a sport.

An even better idea is to telnet to a BBS. Assuming you are connected to the Internet with a local telephone number, you can avoid long-distance telephone costs.

If you can discover the host name (example: boardwatch.littleton.co.us) or the IP (Internet Protocol) address (example: 199.33.229.254) of a BBS, you can telnet to that bulletin board because it has an Internet address.

Many, but not all, BBSes have Internet access. The way to find out is to first log in normally to a particular BBS through your communications program. Does the BBS have Internet access? What is its host name or IP address? Then log out and telnet back through your Internet service provider.

PRIVATE SECTOR JOBS

BBS
Free

Private Sector

America's Job Bank

A free nationwide selection of some 100,000 jobs in the private and public sectors (mostly private) compiled by the U.S. Department of Labor from the nation's public employment service offices. Jobs included are those that have gone unfilled in the originating state for several days. The jobs run the full range, from professional and managerial to blue-collar and entry-level. In many areas, the data are dispensed through touchscreen kiosks in shopping malls and other public facilities, but the new Internet accessibility that is planned will make this databank a powerful job-hunting tool.

Sometime soon, America's Job Bank will be available via World Wide Web (see Chapter 3). Additionally, a number of states are in the blueprint stage of making it available to their computer-using citizens.

America's Job Bank is available in a number of media. Here are three good ways to get at it:

1. The state employment services in Texas (see *Texas hi-T.E.C.,* below). The Texas access is attractive because you can telnet free to it.

2. The New York State Department of Labor. Includes America's Job Bank, plus 50,000 jobs listed by New York employers in an online "package" called *Work Station.*

To access by Telnet through the Rural Assistance Information Network (RAIN), telnet to:

rain.health.state.ny.us

Login:

rain

Select:

Work Station

3. The New York State Department of Labor's Work Station, accessible on the Web.

To access by World Wide Web:

http://ageninfo.tamu.edu/jobs.html

Select:

Comprehensive employment servers
New York State Department of Labor Job Database

Login:

Work

America's Job Bank will become a household name as it expands to many other Internet access points in coming years.

BBS
Commercial

Private Sector

Access Technology Limited
Ireland

Irish Weekly Jobs Bulletin

Technical jobs available in Ireland. Bulletin is e-mailed on a weekly basis to subscribers.

To join mailing list, call +353-21-303388 or e-mail request to

   jobs-request@access.ie

For information on posting vacancies, call +353-21-303377 or e-mail information to

   jobs-submit@access.ie

(The plus sign before the numbers means you are to add the numbers of your carrier. If, for example, you are using AT&T, you dial 011 before either number. If you're puzzled, ask a telephone operator for further assistance.)

BBS
Commercial

Private Sector

Argus Virtual Classifieds
Lexington, MA

Nationwide listings, mostly for technical MIS/DP[1] jobs, but including all occupations, such as accountants, buyers, space planners, copywriters, international marketers, environmental engineers, and marketing trainers. Most jobs to date are on the East Coast, from New Hampshire to Florida. The database can be searched by keywords. Jobs are listed in quick one-liners for each position, but each

---

[1] **NOTE:** The term "MIS/DP" appears frequently in this chapter. MIS means management information systems; DP means data processing. Both refer to popular career fields.

can be viewed in detail to learn the definition of skills and the experience and educational requirements. Operated by Computer-Based Communications, the service is free to job seekers; employers pay. Voice: 617-674-2354.

617-674-2345 or **617-674-2761**

To obtain Argus job listings by ftp (through a public Gopher) using binary files, call Argus and ask for directions. Once you understand how to do it, you can download them for free.

BBS
Free

Private Sector

Career Connections
San Francisco, CA

Worldwide job listings. Focus on MIS/DP that can be searched by company, discipline, and geography.

415-903-5815

BBS
Free

Private Sector/Government

Careers Miami
Miami, FL

A job listing of private sector and federal jobs.

305-828-5697

BBS
Free

Private Sector

Career Resource Center
Seattle, WA

Private sector jobs and information resources related to the job search process.

206-706-8217

BBS
Free

Private Sector/Title Insurance Jobs

Condell Online
Hilton Head, SC

Both a job database and a resume database for the insurance field, primarily title insurance. Also includes E-Span job database.

803-686-3465

BBS
Free

Private Sector/Construction Management

Contractors Exchange
San Francisco, CA

Construction/contractor job listings. Updated daily.

415-334-7393

BBS
Commercial

Private Sector

Delight The Customer
Hudsonville, MI

Job listings for quality control, sales, marketing, training, and customer service fields. Also contains a resume database.

616-662-0393

BBS
Free

Private Sector

Digital X-Connect
Plano, TX

Home of JobNet (see p. 91). Contains job opportunity lists nationwide and job-related information. Has listing of all BBSes that carry JobNet service.

214-517-8443

BBS
Free

Private Sector

ECCO*BBS
Chicago, IL
New York (Metro), NY
San Francisco, CA

National, permanent, and contract job listings.

312-404-8685	Chicago
212-580-4510	New York
415-331-7227	San Francisco

BBS
Free

Private Sector

Employment Board
San Diego, CA

JOBS-NOW echo and employment information for the San Diego area.

619-689-1348

BBS
Free

Private Sector

Employment Connection
Leominster, MA

Focuses on jobs at Massachusetts Institute of Technology and in Boston area. Includes resume database. Files include job search information for people with disabilities. Special facilities for visually impaired callers.

508-537-1862

BBS
Free

Private Sector

Employment Connection
Seattle, WA

Accesses Help-Wanted U.S.A. database of jobs, federal jobs, and Internet postings. Includes resume database. (No association with above service in Massachusetts; was being tested at press time.)

206-720-7165

BBS
Commercial

Private Sector

Executive Connection
Dallas, TX

Based in Dallas, this service has a large database of job listings of interest to many.

214-306-3393

BBS
Free

Private Sector

Exec-PC
Green Bay, WI

Based in Wisconsin; contains job listings across the nation, often with descriptions. Includes nontech jobs, such as openings in entertainment and media.

414-789-4210

NetNote

Rave Review

"For one-stop shoppers, the best source I have found is *Executive Connection* in Dallas (e-mail: staff@execon.metronet.com). They have compiled a listing of most BBS systems . . . and offer a free trial of 14 days with 30 minutes per day usage," says G.B., a sales and marketing executive on the prowl for new job connections.

This unsolicited testimonial came to me over the Net. I have withheld G.B.'s name to protect job-search privacy.

BBS
Commercial

Private Sector/Government

First Step
Atlanta, GA

Federal, state, and Internet job listings. Lots of local jobs. Includes resume database.

404-642-0665

BBS
Commercial

Private Sector

Georgia On-Line
Rosewell, GA

A variety of job listings and resume databases.

404-591-0777

BBS
Free
Commercial

Private Sector

Global Trade Net
San Francisco, CA

A board with an international flavor; contains job listings but also useful for international entrepreneurship.

415-668-0422

BBS
Commercial

Private Sector

Index System
Atlanta, GA

Described as a grapevine jobs network with a local jobs base. Includes Internet listings. System is assisting personnel provider for the 1996 Summer Olympic Games in Atlanta.

706-613-0566

BBS
Free

Private Sector

InfoMat
San Clemente, CA

Job opportunity and franchise information.

714-492-8727

BBS
Commercial

Private Sector

IntelliMatch
San Jose, CA

Nationwide opportunities in hardware engineering, software development, marketing, sales, MIS, accounting, and finance. Free to job seekers for first six months. Involves downloading vendor-provided software. Monday through Friday, voice: 800-964-6282.

BBS
Free

Private Sector

Job and Opportunity Link
Chicago, IL

A variety of job ads that can be downloaded.

708-690-9860

BBS
Commercial

Private Sector

Jobbs
Roswell, GA

Recruiter-sponsored (Alpha Systems, a contingency search firm). Positions for all functions in the Southeast region of the United States. Also has listings of recruiting firms. Includes resume database. Upload resume to join applicant pool now and for the future.

404-992-8937

BBS
Free

Private Sector

Jobs
Portland, OR

A good source for jobs nationwide. Home of the moderator of the JOBS-NOW echo. Updated daily.

503-281-6808

BBS
Free
Commercial

Private Sector

Job Search Board
Ontario, Canada

Both job and resume databases. Additional services available for a fee.

416-588-3821

BBS
Free

Private Sector

Job Trac
Dallas, TX

Focus is on local and state positions—all types. Also includes resume database.

214-349-0527

BBS
Commercial

Private Sector

Online Opportunities
Philadelphia, PA

Source of all types of jobs in the Pennsylvania Tri-State area. Includes the Help Wanted USA database and resume database.

215-873-7170 and **610-873-7170**

BBS
Free

Private Sector

Opportunity
Hampton Roads, VA

A source of regional positions of all types in the Southeast. Includes resume database.

804-588-4031

BBS
Commercial

Private Sector

Tag On-Line Career Bank
Philadelphia, PA

Covers the nation in vacancies for all functions and industries. Includes resume database.

215-969-3845

BBS
Free

Private Sector

Texas hi-T.E.C.
Austin, TX
Texas Employment Commission

An automated bulletin board that not only showcases both private and public jobs in Texas, but is an Internet access to America's Job Bank, a 100,000-position database operated by the U.S. Department of Labor. (Other state employment services soon will arrange Internet access to America's Job Bank.)

The hi-T.E.C. computerized public access service carries information to the public about the Texas Employment Commission (TEC) services, Texas labor laws, and job opportunities throughout the state, including the Governor's Job Bank, a database of Texas state agency job postings.

To access by Telnet:

hi-tec.tec.state.tx.us

Texas residents can access the service free by calling through the State Comptroller's bulletin board, then requesting on the menu of choices, to be patched through to hi-T.E.C. The number to call is:

800-227-8392

Callers outside Texas will have to pay individual long-distance tolls to complete their calls. Access hi-T.E.C. by setting your communications software to No Parity, 8 databits, 1 stopbit, Full Duplex, and VT100 terminal emulation (N,8,1,F, VT100) and dialing:

512-475-4893

BBS
Basic Free (mostly) with small fees

Private Sector

The Data Dimension PCBoard
Duluth, GA

Various jobs in Atlanta. Not a commercial board, but small fees are needed to defray costs.

404-495-9479

BBS
Commercial

Private Sector

The People's X-Change
Somerville, NJ

Services include job listings, as well as a resume database and student profile database. A new addition is Japanese databases.
Voice: 908-685-1900.

909-685-0948

To access by Telnet:

csii.com

TECHNICAL JOBS

BBS
Free

Technical Jobs

Advanced R&D
Orlando, FL

Company-sponsored board; temporary job assignments. MIS/DP positions. Resumes solicited; upload.

407-894-0580

BBS
Free

Technical Jobs

Analysts International Corp.
Dallas, TX

Company-sponsored board. Contract MIS/DP positions. Resumes solicited; upload.

214-263-9161

BBS
Free

Technical Jobs

Career Systems Online
Springfield, MA

Variety of jobs, including opportunities nationwide.

413-592-9208

BBS
Commercial

Technical Jobs

Careers First, Inc.
Atlantic City, NJ

Free to job seekers; operated by a technical recruiter of computer personnel. Focus is on a tri-state area: Pennsylvania, New Jersey, and Delaware. One of the pioneer job boards.

609-786-2666

BBS
Free

Technical Jobs

Careers Online
Andover, MA

Computerworld's board with listings of jobs published in the newspaper.

508-879-4700

BBS
Free

Technical Jobs

Computer Careers
Charlotte, NC

Operated by EDP Professionals, Inc. Specializes in data processing jobs nationwide.

704-554-1102

BBS
Free

Technical Jobs

Data Processing Network
San Francisco, CA

Recruiter-sponsored (Toner Corp., a contingency search firm) database of data processing jobs for the San Francisco/Sacramento area. Upload resume for consideration for current and future vacancies. Limited access without resume upload. JOBS-NOW echo, in the Information Services section, has listings of data processing jobs nationwide. Updated daily.

415-788-8663

BBS
Free

Technical Jobs

D.I.C.E. National Network
Chicago, IL
Des Moines, IA
Dallas, TX
Newark, NJ
Sunnyvale, CA

A nationwide board headquartered in Des Moines, Iowa, and currently in five cities. Designed for both contract and permanent MIS/DP positions. Job posting from 80+ companies, employment agencies, and recruiters. Updated several times daily. Each board has same listings, so only call one system.

708-782-0960	Chicago, IL
515-280-3423	Des Moines, IA
214-691-3420	Dallas, TX
201-242-4166	Newark, NJ
408-737-9339	Sunnyvale, CA

To access by Telnet:

dice.com

BBS
Free

Technical Jobs

Data Processing Centers' The Computer Jobs
Ft. Worth, TX

Recruiter-sponsored (Data Processing Centers, a contingency search firm). Recruiter solicits data processing resumes. At press time, connection problems occurred because of line sharing.

817-268-2193

BBS
Free

Technical Jobs

DP Job Works
Ft. Wayne, IN

Recruiter-sponsored (DP Job Works, a contingency search firm). Specializing in data processing positions nationwide, includes resume database. Upload resume to join applicant pool now and in the future.

219-436-9702

BBS
Free

Technical Jobs

Enginet
Fairfield, OH

A job service for engineers and their employers.

513-858-2688

BBS
Free

Technical Jobs

Fortune Consultants of Orlando
Orlando, FL

Operated by a contingency search firm specializing in technical and engineering positions.

407-875-1028

BBS
Free

Technical Jobs

Robert Half
Atlanta, GA

Recruiter-sponsored (Robert Half, a contingency search firm). Specializes in MIS/DP positions. Includes resume database. Upload a resume to join applicant pool for current and future openings.

404-392-0540

BBS
Free

Technical Jobs

ISCA
Atlanta, GA

A small job listing service of the Information Systems Consultant Association.

404-491-1335

BBS
Free

Technical Jobs

J-Connection
Atlanta, GA
South Florida
Washington, DC (metro area)

A job listing of permanent and contract MIS/DP jobs. Positions organized by region. Features frequent updates.

404-662-5500	Atlanta
813-791-0101	South Florida
703-379-0553	Washington, DC area

BBS
Free

Technical Jobs

Job Bulletin Board
Dallas, TX

Recruiter-sponsored (recruiter for Technical Recruiting Associates, a contingency search firm specializing in high-tech positions). Features local MIS/DP positions.

214-612-9925

BBS
Free

Technical Jobs

Lee Johnson
Crockette, CA

Recruiter-sponsored (Lee Johnson, an executive recruiter). Specializes in software engineering jobs. Resumes solicited; upload.

510-787-3191

BBS
Free

Technical Jobs

KJA Associates
Edina, MN

Recruiter-sponsored (Kasta, James and Associates, a contingency executive recruiting firm). Specializes in MIS jobs. Includes resume database. Upload resume.

612-536-0533

BBS
Free

Technical Jobs

MacEast
Boston, MA

Jobs listings span the United States and abroad, with emphasis on listings for the Northeast. Includes conferences (interest groups) and Usenet newsgroups.

617-899-0020

BBS
Free

Technical Jobs

New Professional Network
Amherst, MA

Recruiter-sponsored (Allen Davis & Assoc., a contingency search firm). Focuses on MIS/DP positions nationwide. Includes resume database. Offers forums and career guides. Solicits resumes; upload.

413-549-8136

BBS
Free

Technical Jobs

Opportunity Mart
Wakefield, MA

Company-sponsored board. Contract MIS/DP positions. Resumes solicited; upload.

617-246-8243

BBS
Commercial

Technical Jobs

Reunions USA
Asbury Park, NJ

Jobs for technical personnel.

908-741-9460

BBS
Free

Technical Jobs

Society For Technical Communications
Washington, DC

Operated by The Society For Technical Communications, for technical writers. Job listings available only to verified STC members.

703-522-3299

BBS
Free
Commercial

Technical Jobs

The Polymer Wire, Inc.
Cedar Springs, MI

A nationwide database for the plastics and chemical industry. Jobs and small business opportunities.

616-696-7777

Under Construction

BBS
Nonprofit Organization

American Institute of Architects
AIA Employment Referrals
Washington, DC

An online bulletin board that is being established by the AIA's Online Computer Network. A planned $5 signup fee (for AIA members) and 15 cents a minute will allow viewing at least 40 to 50 job openings for architects and job seekers in related fields. For information,

800-864-7753

GOVERNMENT JOBS

BBS
Free

Government Jobs

AVADS
Washington, DC

Automated Vacancy Announcement Distribution System; lists job vacancies at the Department of Interior.

800-368-3321

BBS
Free

Government Jobs

Cap Access Career Center
Washington, DC

The National Capital Area Public Access Network, Inc.; contains job information for the National Institutes of Health, National Science Foundation, and other federal government agencies.

To access:

Login:

> Guest

Password:

> Visitor

> **202-785-1523**

To access by Telnet:

> cap.gwu.edu

Login:

> Guest

Password:

> Visitor

Type:

> go careers

BBS
Free

Government Jobs

Census Personnel Board
Suitland, MD

Operated by the U.S. Department of Commerce's Bureau of the Census. Job listings for Suitland only.

> **301-763-4574**

BBS
Free

Government Jobs

Detroit Service Center
Detroit, MI

Operated by the U.S. Office of Personnel Management. Contains federal job opportunity lists and information for the Detroit region.

313-226-4423

BBS
Free

Government Jobs

Federal Jobline
Los Angeles, CA

An electronic Federal Job Information Center operated by the Office of Personnel Management. Contains federal job listings and information for the Western Region.

818-575-6521

BBS
Free

Government Jobs

FJOB
Federal Job Opportunity Board
Macon, GA

Federal Job Information Center operated by the Office of Personnel Management. Contains federal job listings and information for all of the United States, plus a listing of government job fairs across the country.

912-757-3100

To access by Telnet:

fjob.mail.opm.gov

BBS
Free

Government Jobs

Job Watch
Schenectady, NY

Federal jobs, organized by region.

518-393-3826

BBS
Free

Government Jobs/Maryland State

LGPA
Local Government Personnel Association
Baltimore, MD

A database of Maryland State jobs, available for downloading. Works on easy-to-use Wildcat system.

410-333-7221

BBS
Free

Government Jobs: Criminal Justice Professionals

NELS
National Employment Listing Service Bulletin

No longer available in print form; an online listing that focuses exclusively on jobs in the criminal justice field. Contains up-to-date national employment listings for all types of criminal justice jobs, including law enforcement and corrections personnel. Published by the Criminal Justice Center at Sam Houston State University, Huntsville, TX. Available on the Search bulletin board, operated by a nonprofit justice organization in Sacramento, CA. After completing the online registration process, find the NELS Catalog in the database section of the main menu. If difficult to log on, call the Search Group; voice: 916-392-2550.

916-392-4640

Also available by ftpmail, which is ftp (file transfer protocol, see Chapter 3) via e-mail. The advantage: avoid long-distance charges when downloading a file of substantial information.

To access NELS by ftpmail, send an e-mail message to:

ftpmail@search.org

Type:

get nels_cat.txt

(A copy of the NELS catalog will be sent within 24 hours by e-mail. The catalog runs between 20 and 60 pages. You can print it, or just look at it on your computer screen.)

BBS
Free

Government Jobs

OPM FedJobs—Philly
Philadelphia, PA

Operated by the U.S. Office of Personnel Management; the source for open federal government jobs and training schedules for all of the United States. Updated daily.

215-580-2216

BBS
Free

Government Jobs

OPM Mainstreet
Washington, DC

Operated by the U.S. Office of Personnel Management. Contains a variety of information for government employees, but is available to anyone. Has a gateway to the other Federal Job Information Centers.

202-606-4800

BBS
Free

Government Jobs

Nebraska Online!
State jobs in Nebraska.

800-392-7932

BBS
Free

Government Jobs/Education

Texas Education Agency
Austin, TX

A list of education-related job vacancies in Texas. See Texas hi-T.E.C., under Private Sector Jobs, for directions on reaching it. Or, call directly.

512-475-3689

JOBNET BULLETIN BOARDS

JobNet, which is both a job database and a resume database bulletin board service, was created by Andrew Walding in Plano, Texas. Launched in 1993, JobNet is, at this time, a free service to job hunters and employers. More than 100 bulletin boards with local telephone numbers now carry JobNet.

Most of the BBSes carrying JobNet are multi-interest boards; employment topics are only part of their offerings. Within JobNet are multiple conferences (interest groups).

Some BBSes carrying JobNet are listed above because they are totally or somewhat employment focused.

Given below is a selection of more JobNet bulletin boards—those we accessed on the first try (a good sign). Some BBSes only operate between 10 P.M. and 4 A.M.

Because it is less costly to make local rather than long-distance calls, the boards are arranged in alphabetical order by the city in which they are based.

Selected JobNet BBS Affiliates

Alice, TX **Jacob's House**	**512-664-7570**
Ambler, PA **UnNamed**	**215-540-0141**
Austin, TX **Camel's Back**	**512-243-0077**
Bellbrook, OH **Authors' Area**	**513-848-4288**
Blythe, GA **The Imperial Palace**	**706-592-1344**
Brick, NJ **The H.E.S.**	**908-840-6921**
Canoga Park, CA **Jobbs 'n Stuff**	**818-999-0928**
Capistrano Beach, CA **The Big Blue Mac**	**714-493-4779**
Cedar Park, TX **DataSource**	**512-219-6629**
Clearwater, FL **The BizBoard Info. Svcs.**	**813-532-4473**
Colleyville, TX **Electronics Unlimited**	**817-267-5393**
Coram, NY **The Silicon Garden**	**516-736-6662**
Cranford, NJ **The Vector**	**908-276-4405**
Crumm Lynne, PA **Storm Front**	**215-788-4662**
Dallas, TX **The Lonesome Dove**	**214-355-1835**
Dallas, TX **Planet**	**214-306-8269**
Darby, PA **The Seekers Place**	**215-237-1281**
Denton, TX **Terminal Delusions**	**817-565-8437**

Denville, NJ
Mt Hed   **201-625-1519**

Duncanville, TX
Texstar   **214-298-0273**

Elmhurst, NY
Jim's PC Paradise   **718-458-0502**

Embden, ME
Mike's Embden   **207-566-5737**

Fitzwilliam, NH
More Byte For The Buck   **603-585-3326**

Fort Wayne, IN
The Midwest Connection   **219-432-6351**

Fremont, CA
The Smorgasbord   **510-440-1125**

Granada Hills, CA
The MOG-UR'S EMS   **818-366-1238**

Hampden, MA
The Birds Nest   **413-566-2424**

Hayward, CA
Bust Out   **510-888-1443**

Highland, VA
Falcon's Crest   **804-730-2492**

Las Vegas, NV
Classic Image   **702-247-6393**

Los Angeles, CA
Link   **310-459-1264**

Los Angeles, CA
Thundervolts   **213-225-5474**

Los Fresnos, TX
Newberry   **210-233-3312**

Louisville, KY
The Realm Infoservices   **502-254-7036**

Maryland, MO
NeverLand   **314-579-9369**

Norton AFB, CA
The Irish Connection   **909-888-3655**

Oceanside, CA
Compu-Tronics   **619-430-1142**

Philadelphia, PA
Perry-1 Host Systems   215-698-7677

Philadelphia, TN
The Nite-Lite   615-458-9099

Plano, TX
The BucketBored!   214-414-6913

Poughkeepsie, NY
The Outer Limit   914-462-0363

Red Bank, NJ
The Red Shift   908-224-0181

Reston, VA
World Data Network   703-648-1841

Richardson, TX
The Lunatic Fringe   214-235-5288

San Clemente, CA
InfoMat   714-492-8727

San Diego, CA
The Business Connection   619-576-0049

San Diego, CA
Grizz's Domain   619-538-2693

Silver Spring, MD
Deaf New World   301-587-2277

Simi Valley, CA
The Resume File   805-581-6210

Spring Hill, FL
Drum Corps USA   904-666-8405

Stafford, VA
Hils Haus   703-680-7112

Standish, ME
Maine Career Connection   207-642-4802

Syracuse, NJ
Tony's Place   315-428-3373

Upper Darby, PA
Punch Into The Future   215-352-0413

Victoria, TX
The Round Table   512-578-4482

Vista, CA
The Outer Dimension   619-724-1931

JobNet Conferences

JobNet, in its mission to provide job seekers and employers a place to find each other, has established conferences (interest groups).

Job Listings

Employers post openings in these groups:

Accounting and financial
Administrative/clerical
Contract and temporary
Engineering, chemical
Engineering, electrical & electronic
Engineering, environmental
Engineering, mechanical
Engineering, miscellaneous
Health and medical
Human resources
International
Local positions only (state of BBS location)
Miscellaneous
Multiple (volume openings not classified)
Professional and managerial
Purchasing, buying, and contracts
Sales and marketing
Software related
Technical writing and kindred
Technical, general

Resume Listings

Job seekers post resumes in these groups:

Administrative and clerical
Miscellaneous
Professional and managerial
Technical and engineering

Job and Career Fairs

Nationwide calendar and discussion of job and career fairs.

Job Search Topics

Several conferences offer an exchange of ideas on topics of interest to job seekers:

General mail and problem solving
Interviewing advice, stories, experiences
Job seeking advice, personal stories

Washington, DC
The CPA's   **202-882-9067**

Woodbridge, VA
Crossroads   **703-590-0049**

Yeadon, PA
Attic Treasures   **610-394-9565**

JOBS YOU REACH BY NEWSGROUPS

Assuming you're hooked up to the Internet with a local telephone connection, newsgroups may be an early port of call for job shopping.

You can get to newsgroups in several ways, including commercial online services, and through your Internet service provider where you make choices through the provider's menu system.

Usenet, mentioned briefly in Chapter 3, is a global conferencing system that pulls in a variety of entities—private sector organizations, government, universities, home computers.

The idea is to exchange "news" by writing it and reading it. On some newsgroups, you can read about job vacancies or post your resume; on others, you have to be indirect. You may simply ask for "referrals" or for general ideas about the job market in a specific geographic locale.

NetNote

BBS Lists

BBSes come and go. To locate a local bulletin board system in your area, you can call the User Group Locator Hotline: telephone 914-876-6678. To obtain free lists compiled from a number of sources, try the ftp route.

To request by anonymous ftp:

    oak.oakland.edu

Select:

    /pub/misc/bbslists

Usenet newsgroups are similar in their potential for interactive discussion to mailing lists, but, as mentioned earlier, there are a few differences.

With mailing lists, each person who has subscribed sees every message.

On Usenet, every message (newsgroup "article") is received and stored on each participating Usenet computer, instead of being sent to each person. If you want to read the articles in the newsgroup, you must choose the newsgroup. *Even when you do not participate in a given newsgroup on an ongoing basis, you can still access all of its articles.*

Newsgroups are organized in a topical hierarchical system. (See Figure 4–1.) There are seven big Usenet categories and a number of "alternative" categories. (Some experts say there are 20 or more categories and the number grows constantly.)

Of an estimated 14,000 newsgroups, fewer than 2,500 are worldwide. The big seven Usenet hierarchies are usually carried at all the Usenet

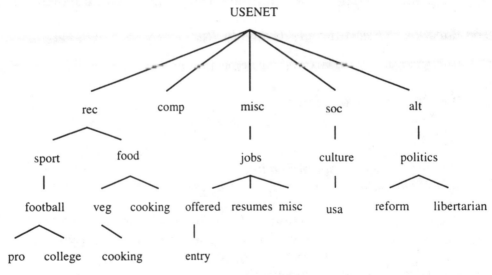

The diagram above is a partial map of the USENET hierarchy. It contains the following groups:

- rec.sport.football.pro
- rec.sport.footbal.college
- rec.food.veg.cooking
- rec.food.cooking
- misc.jobs.offered
- misc.jobs.offered.entry
- misc.jobs.resumes
- misc.jobs.misc
- soc.culture.usa
- alt.politics.reform
- alit.politics.libertarian

Figure 4–1   Example of USENET Hierarchy

sites, but not all sites carry the alternative groups. An alternative news-group can be created by anyone with the technical skill to set it up, which is why they are rated "alternative."

Job hunters chiefly are interested in the *misc* and *alt* categories, but you'll also want to check the groups that are in or related to your career field, such as *sci.geo.meteorology* (discussion of meteorology) or *biz.books.technical* (buying and selling books; book reviews; business news).

To read or post to newsgroups, you need *news reader software.* This avoids one-by-one sifting to find out what's out there. You do not need to send e-mail to a group administrator; just use the software to subscribe to newsgroups you select.

The reader program organizes the newsgroups for you, displays the articles—job listings or related career information—you request, and gives you the ability to post articles (resumes).

You usually can use news reader programs provided by your Internet service provider, system administrator, or commercial online service. If you have trouble operating an old and creaky news reader, you may be able to find one you like better. New and improved news readers appear regularly. Some are free for the downloading. Two examples are:

For Macintosh: "NewsWatcher." Obtain by ftp:

ftp.acns.nwu.edu (in the /pub/newswatcher)

For Dos: "trumpet." Obtain by ftp:

oak.oakland.edu

Tracy LaQuey, author of *The Internet Companion: A Beginner's Guide to Global Networking* (see the Appendix) says it is a good idea to lurk before you leap.

"The first thing you should do is read all the articles in the *news.announce.newusers* newsgroup. These articles will get you up to speed. If, after reading, you still have questions, post them to the *news.newusers.questions* newsgroup."

Use good judgment when you post your resume, LaQuey advises. "It's probably not the best idea to post your resume to *rec.folk-dancing.*"

If you want a broader tutorial on newsgroups, read Eric Gagnon's *What's on the Internet,* or Jenny A. Fristrup's *Usenet: Newnews for Everyone* (see the Appendix).

Job-Related Newsgroups

This selection of key job-related newsgroups was identified by my researchers.

atl.jobs
> Jobs available and jobs wanted, Atlanta, GA.

atl.resumes
> Resume postings in Atlanta, GA.

Austin.jobs
> Jobs in Austin, TX.

aus.ads.jobs
aus.jobs
> Two Australian groups: jobs available and jobs wanted.

ba.jobs.contract
> Contract employment issues in San Francisco (Bay Area), CA.

ba.jobs.misc
> Discussion about the job market in the San Francisco Bay Area.

ba.jobs.offered
> Job postings in the San Francisco Bay Area.

balt.jobs
> Job offerings in the Baltimore/Washington, DC area

bionet.jobs
> Job discussions for professional biologists.

biz.jobs.offered
> Position announcements for computer software/hardware and electrical engineering jobs. Most are from technical recruiting firms.

bln.jobs
> Germany: Jobs in Berlin. German language.

can.jobs
> Jobs in Canada.

chi.jobs
> Jobs in Chicago.

cle.jobs
> Jobs in Cleveland.

comp.sys.next.marketplace
> NeXT hardware, software, and jobs.

dc.jobs
> Jobs in the Washington, DC metro area.

de.markt.jobs
> Jobs in Germany; must use German language.

dk.jobs
> Jobs in Denmark.

dod.jobs
> Department of Defense job postings.

fl.jobs
> Jobs in Florida.

hepnet.jobs
> Job announcements and discussions for high-energy and nuclear physics research.

houston.jobs.offered
> Jobs in Houston.

hsv.jobs
> Jobs in Huntsville, AL.

ia.jobs
> Jobs in Iowa.

ie.jobs
> Jobs in Ireland.

il.jobs.misc
> Jobs in Illinois.

il.jobs.offered
> Available jobs in the Illinois area.

il.jobs.resumes
> Resume postings for the Illinois area.

in.jobs
> Jobs available in Indiana.

kw.jobs
> Jobs in Canada (Kitchener & Waterloo).

la.jobs
> Jobs in Los Angeles.

mi.jobs
> Jobs in Michigan.

milw.jobs
> Jobs in Milwaukee.

misc.jobs.contract
> Ads for short-term contract software development jobs, technical writing jobs, and specialized CAD operation positions.

misc.jobs.misc
> Discussion about employment, workplace, careers. Recommended for getting career ideas and interviewing tips, as well as getting inside information on what it's like to work for specific companies. This newsgroup is not for posting resumes or jobs.

misc.jobs.offered
> For employers to post non-entry-level opportunities. General positions available.

misc.jobs.offered.entry
> Job listings only for entry-level positions. No discussion. Help-wanted listings for entry-level positions—such as customer service reps, sales reps, and part-time jobs—in high-tech companies.

misc.jobs.resumes
> Postings of resumes. ASCII format only. Also includes requests for jobs wanted.

e.jobs
> Jobs in New England.

ont.jobs
> Jobs in Ontario, Canada.

ott.jobs
> Jobs in Ottawa, Canada.

osu.jobs
> Jobs at Ohio State University.

sci.research.careers
> Issues relevant to careers in scientific research.

sdnet.jobs
> Jobs in San Diego.

seattle jobs.offered
> Jobs in Seattle.

stl.jobs
> St. Louis job information.

swnet.jobs
> Jobs in Sweden.

tor.jobs
> Jobs in Toronto, Ontario, Canada.

triangle.jobs
> Jobs in the Research Triangle Park area of North Carolina—Raleigh, Durham, and Chapel Hill.

tx.jobs
> Jobs in Texas.

ucb.jobs
> Jobs at University of California, Berkeley.

ucd.kiosk.jobs
> Jobs at University of California, Davis.

uiuc.cs.jobs
uiuc.misc.jobs
uiuc.kiosk.jobs
> Three groups: jobs at University of Illinois at Urbana-Champaign.

uk.jobs
> Jobs wanted in United Kingdom. No discussions.

uk.jobs.d
> Discussion of job-related issues in United Kingdom.

uk.jobs.offered
> Jobs vacant in United Kingdom. No discussion.

uk.jobs.wanted
> Situations wanted. No discussion.

umn.cs.jobs
umn.general.jobs
umn.itlab.jobs
> Three groups: jobs at University of Minnesota.

us.jobs.contract
> Contract positions in the United States.

us.jobs.misc
> Miscellaneous jobs in the United States.

us.jobs.offered
> Jobs offered in the United States.

us.jobs.offered.entry
> Entry-level positions offered in the United States.

us.jobs.resumes
> Resume posting for positions in the United States.

ut.jobs
> Jobs vacant and wanted at University of Texas.

vmsnet.employment
> Jobs sought/offered, workplace-and employment-related issues.
> (Moderated.)

za.ads.jobs
> Jobs in South Africa.

NetNote

Selected Usenet Categories

The Big 7

comp	Computer discussions.
misc	Job hunting and other topics that don't fit elsewhere.
news	Groups dealing with Usenet software and network administration.
rec	Recreational subjects and hobbies.
sci	Science: space research, math, logic, physics.
soc	Socializing or discussing social issues.
talk	Long discussions, debates—politics, religion, the environment, and so forth.

Sampling of Alternative Categories

alt	Alternative discussions not carried by all Usenet sites.
bionet	Biology topics, including job opportunities in biology.
biz	Discussion groups about businesses.
ddn	U.S. Department of Defense issues.
ieee	Electrical and electronic engineering issues.
info	Technical groups, ranging from Computer Emergency Response Team to Women in Science and Engineering Network.
k12	Education groups with a focus on grades kindergarten through high school.

JOBS YOU REACH BY GOPHER

Countless free job resources can be tapped by gophering to various sites. Although the trend is toward putting Gopher sites on the World Wide Web, a number are listed here as Gopher-accessible because that's how most people learned about them.

SELECTED UNIVERSITIES WITH ONLINE POWER

A number of colleges and universities have already done the cyberspace work to facilitate online career decisionmaking and job hunting possible.

At Michigan State University in East Lansing, Dr. Patrick Sheetz, an adviser to this book, has created **Michigan State University Gopher,** an impressive Gopher file for use by undergraduates, graduating students, and alumni.

The file offers information on a wide range of topics, from campus interview instructions and resume preparation to job vacancies and questions to expect from employers. Career fairs are noted, and a referral directory of the university's schools is available.

If you want to see how complete such a Gopher can be, telnet to:

gopher.msu.edu

Another impressive resource is the **West Georgia College Jobnet** service, a collection of job opportunities and career guidance literature.

WGC Jobnet includes such topics as employment opportunities within the United States and around the globe. Designed to serve a wide audience, it is particularly helpful to college students and faculty. WGC Jobnet offers jobs by subject, such as collections sponsored by the American Mathematical Society and other professional groups; general

---

NetNote

Crossposting Your Resume

To cover a wider area when posting your resume or other messages on newsgroups, try the technique of *crossposting.*

Crossposting allows a single message to be posted on multiple newsgroups without taking up space and valuable resources by posting on each newsgroup individually.

To crosspost, simply list the newsgroups, separated only by a comma (no space) between newsgroups, in the header of your message. Here is an example:

Newsgroup: ba.jobs.offered,misc. jobs.offered,dc.jobs

Make sure you are posting messages in the correct newsgroups. Crossposting may annoy some people; if you crosspost to an incorrect newsgroup, duck for cover as the flames come roaring in.

hiring tips; and links to a wide variety of additional job databases accessible by various Gophers world-wide. Jobnet is on Telnet and on most public Gopher sites.

Telnet to:

131.144.4.9

Login:

info

Password:

info

Select:

#10 for Selected Gophers
#1 Univ. System of Ga. Gopher Servers
#13 West Georgia College
#2 Jobnet

NetNote

Going to Gopher

A reminder: You can connect to Gopher through your local system Gopher, or you can telnet to one of these public Gopher sites:

consultant.micro.umn.edu
seymour.md.gov
gopher.uiuc.edu
gopher.msu.edu
sunsite.unc.edu

For each of these sites, the login name is "Gopher."

More Gopher Resources

Academic Medicine

Academic Physician and Scientist

More than 400 positions in academic medicine, from 126 medical schools and affiliated teaching hospitals, make this the largest online database of its kind. Jobs include administration, basic science, clinical science, and openings with the Food and Drug Administration. You can browse by specialty, location, or keywords.

To access by Gopher:

    aps.acad-phy-sci.com

All Jobs

Online Career Center

The Online Career Center, headquartered in Indianapolis, Indiana, is a nonprofit employer association that provides a variety of career-related services; Employers pay; job seekers can use it free, although a modest charge may be made to enter your resume into the database if you provide it on paper rather than electronically.

The Online Career Center database is operated by IQuest Network Services, an Internet service provider in Indianapolis, Indiana. All types of jobs are carried. Send your resume electronically in ASCII (universal computer language); it will be kept for 90 days, and you can extend the retention until you are employed. Search job openings by keywords, job title, company name, or geographical region.

This premier online service is growing even as you read these lines. In 1993, about 20,000 accesses (inquiries by both employers and jobseekers) were made; in 1995, the figure is running in excess of 4 million accesses, says its executive director, William O. Warren.

Online Career Center can be reached in various ways, including through most commercial online services, and on the Web.

To access by Gopher:

    occ.com

Select:

    The Online Career Center

To access by World Wide Web:

    http://www.occ.com/occ/

or

    http://occ.com/

To obtain information by e-mail:

    occ-info@occ.com

All Jobs

Job Search and Employment Opportunities: Best Bets from the Net

This resource is not a listing of job openings, but a "list of listings." Created by Bradley Leland Taylor and Philip Ray, it is maintained by the University of Michigan's School of Information and Library Studies. The list is an excellent contribution to job search literature and has become part of the university's Clearinghouse for Subject-Oriented Internet Resource Guides. It is available free by Gopher or World Wide Web.

    The list is called "Best Bets" because it does not attempt to be comprehensive, but makes selective judgments. Inclusion in the guide is based on a review of the resource's comprehensiveness, ability to serve the needs of a particular discipline, ease of navigation, timeliness, or overall quality.

To access by Gopher:

    gopher.lib.umich.edu

Select:
    What's New and Featured Resources
    Clearinghouse for Subject-Oriented Internet Resource Guides
    All Guides
    Job Searching and Employment

To access by World Wide Web:

    http://asa.ugl.lib.umich.edu/chdocs/employment/

Economists

Job Openings for Economists
JOE

JOE advertises quite a few jobs, but most are in academe and require a doctorate. Some jobs, business and non-profit organizations, have less rigid educational requirements. JOE is operated by the American Economic Association. You can browse and search to your heart's content.

To access by Gopher:

vuinfo.vanderbilt.edu

Select:
Employment Opportunities
Job Openings for Economists

Education Jobs

Academic Position Network

Job listings include faculty, administrative, and staff jobs in higher education. Some graduate assistant and fellowship positions are noted. Late last year, Bradley Leland Taylor, at the University of Michigan, found 187 jobs from 92 institutions. You can search by keywords, state, or country. Most are in the United States, but Canada and Australia have some current postings. Institutions pay fees to be listed, but the service is free to job seekers.

To access by Gopher:

wcni.cis.umn.edu(port) 11111

Education Jobs

University of Minnesota College of Education's
Job-Search Bulletin Board

Hundreds of job postings for the elementary and secondary grades are carried here. Categories include: administration, media specialty, psychology, counseling, early childhood development, and vocational-technical. Be sure to check under "higher education"—surprisingly, a large number of high school jobs are posted there.

To access by Gopher:

rodent.cis.umn.edu(port) 11119

Federal Jobs

Job Openings in the Federal Government

This is an especially user-friendly Gopher service for searching federal jobs by regional location or government agency. Lots of supplementary materials, such as locality pay tables and occupational requirements, can make you a resident expert on becoming a fed.

To access by Gopher:

gopher.dartmouth.edu

Historians

HNsource

This resource is affiliated with the History Network and the Department of History at the University of Kansas. There are only a few job postings, but it's the only online game in town for historians. As the Net grows, expect to see more jobs listed for humanities and social sciences.

To access by Gopher:

ukanaix.cc.ukans.edu

Select:

hnsource

Nursing

Nightingale

A very helpful resource for nurses, especially for nursing students. Contains information from very basic questions-answers to technical discussions. *Position Announcements* is a directory providing several options, the best of which is *The Nursing Network*.

To access by Gopher:

nightingale.con.utk.edu

Recent College Graduates

Job Hunter

This source is reported to be rich with job openings specifically targeted at recent college graduates. The majority of jobs listed are in the Midwest. Listings are divided by area, e.g., arts, communications and media, or internships, summer jobs, and international jobs. You can search by keywords. Articles, essays and other information on the job search process are available.

To access by Gopher:

mizzou1.missouri.edu 801

(801 refers to port)

JOBS YOU REACH BY WORLD WIDE WEB

When it comes to looking for jobs advertised in full color with graphics, logos, and big type, the Web is "where it's at." Without a doubt, the Web is the Internet's star showcase for jobs and for the people who want them.

New web browsers available on the leading commercial online information services make everything ultra simple. You don't need a URL address—you merely position your mouse on a resource you like (such as Online Career Center), click, and you're there!

All Jobs

Career Magazine

A comprehensive online career resource, which is free to job seekers, human resource managers and career-minded professionals around the world. It's features include job openings, with a database that can be searched by location, job titles, and skills; employer profiles; interactive discussion groups in which job seekers and human resource professionals interact; news and feature articles; and a directory of executive recruiters that can be searched by industry. A large number of jobs are in the fields of accounting, construction, computers, and environment.

To access by World Wide Web:

http://www.careermag.com/careermag/

NetNote

Web Leads to More Colleges

Here are two specific places to search for college-based job data collections, and a place to look for many others. The difference is that these resources can be found on the World Wide Web, (WWW) as well as Gopher, or instead of Gopher.

To access Rice University's Gopher on the WWW:

> http://riceinfo.rice.edu/RiceInfo/Subject.html

To access Texas A&M's Jobs Page on the WWW:

> http://ageninfo.tamu.edu/jobs.html

To use the Web for referrals to many college databases on Gopher, use the same address:

> http://ageninfo.tamu.edu/jobs.html

All Jobs

Career Taxi

Operated by a giant advertising agency that specializes in recruitment advertising, TMP Worldwide, opened this Web resource with a large number of attractions for job seekers and employers alike. Under construction at press time, advertised features include *Job City* for job listings, and *Cindy's Cafe* for advice. As the opening screen invites, "Hop in!"

To access by World Wide Web:

> http://www.iquest.net/Career_Taxi/taxi.html

All Jobs

CareerMosaic

This is a graphically well-designed commercial site on the Web. CareerMosaic is a great resource for both professionals and college students—and not just those in the high-tech areas. Many of

NetNote

Newsflash!

CareerMosaic now offers WAIS (Wide Area Information Server) capacity. This tool allows you to search an index of all job postings on the Internet job BBSes. *WAIS is a great time saver when you are tracking job listings in a specific field anywhere on the Net, not just in CareerMosaic.* (See Chapter 3 for WAIS.)

the employers currently on the service are in high-tech industries, but dozens more employers in financial, health care, retail, and telecommunications industries are "under construction." You can find not only a fairly comprehensive description of each company and how it operates, but also specific job openings with information on the job title and responsibilities, and the required experience. The message to job seekers is: "Let us show you how wonderful we are." Employers and the jobs they offer are located all around the globe.

CareerMosaic is available to those equipped with Windows, Unix, or a Macintosh computer and World Wide Web access. College students can establish forums to exchange e-mail with employees within a company to find out firsthand what it's like to work there. A planned feature will allow potential employees to move from talk into filing an application form. The service is owned by Bernard Hodes Advertising, a human resource communications firm specializing in recruitment and employee communications.

To access by World Wide Web:

http://www.careermosaic.com

All Jobs

CareerWeb

A product of Landmark Communications of Norfolk, Virginia, Career-Web is the newest career service site on the Web. This major resource offers employers and career-related companies the opportunity to describe themselves and to recruit candidates. It offers job seekers a convenient, friendly place to find company profiles, job openings, professional associations, career materials, franchise opportunities, area demographics, and future hiring trends. CareerWeb is expected to become one of the "don't miss" stops on Internet job searches—for local, regional, national, and global positions.

To access by World Wide Web (via Landmark Communications' InfiNet)

http://www.infi.net/

All Jobs

E-Span
Interactive Employment Network

E-Span, Inc., a division of J.B. Laughrey, Inc., in Indianapolis, is a blue-chip, four-year-old national online employment resource for employers and job seekers. It provides electronic advertising, as well as a database of resumes 24 hours a day, seven days a week, through most major commercial online services and bulletin boards across the country.

E-Span customers include Fortune 1000 companies in all industries, search firms, and developmental technical organizations.

Its newest service is the Interactive Employment Network (IEN), which is clothed in an appealing display of color and graphics and is accessible through the Web. IEN provides a fully searchable database of more than 1,000 job openings in data processing, information systems, engineering, manufacturing, government, sciences, finance and accounting, education, human resources, medical, pharmaceutical, and developmental technical organizations.

Also offered are a wide variety of resources for the job seeker, including advice by Marilyn Moats Kennedy and other high-profile career management authors. Some salary guides are available, and the *Occupational Outlook Handbook* can be viewed as well. The service—free to job seekers—can be used with any Web browser. Job seekers also are invited to e-mail (resume@espan3.espan.com) their resumes, or to postal mail paper resumes to E-Span. Human resource managers and recruiters who advertise online with E-Span can access the resume database and respond directly to job seekers.

E-Span is available on several commercial online services, including CompuServe, America Online, GEnie, Exec PC, and IndustryNet. Additional information can be obtained by e-mail (info@espan3.espan.com).

To access by World Wide Web:

http://www.espan.com/

All Jobs

Monster Board

This is a commercial site on the Web operated by Adion Information Services, a large recruitment advertising agency in New England. Free to job seekers, it has specific job openings and entertaining monster graphics to keep you moving through the board.

The Monster Board seems to offer an overview of employers, a "CyberFair" for college and entry-level positions, and a helpful "browse and select" feature that allows you to job search by company name, location, discipline, industry, and specific job title. Most of the jobs thus far are for technical positions, but a number are turning up in marketing, sales, multimedia, and management. There appears to be a growing number of biotechnology and pharmaceutical jobs as well. The vast majority of the jobs are in East Coast locations, chiefly in New England, but a small number are located across the country.

Unique to the career-searching sites on the Web, the Monster Board uses a Mosaic forms application process. Once you target a position, you can apply online with a brief application form, or you can e-mail your entire resume to the appropriate job slot. In either case, all responses are managed at the Monster Board Web site, instead of through the usual method of sending a resume directly to the employer. (Monster Board personnel screen out applicants who are considered unqualified for the target position.) Corporate recruiters have immediate access to the resume postings.

At press time, only about 50 companies were listed on the Monster Board's companies roster, but many more are found in the postings in the career search section.

To access by World Wide Web:

http://www.monster.com/

Business Jobs

Stanford University List—Business: Employment

Stanford University sponsors a wonderful "list of lists"—indicators of a wide range of primary source materials you get somewhere else. You can have a good time just typing the URL (uniform resource locator, a type of Internet address)—yahoo!

To access by World Wide Web:

http://akebono.stanford.edu/yahoo/Business/Employment

Education Jobs

The Chronicle of Higher Education

With nearly 1,000 current positions in higher education and related fields, this resource includes broad categories of faculty and research openings, administrative and executive postings, and jobs outside academe. You can search by keywords, or by U.S. or overseas regions. The Chronicle is also available via World Wide Web.

To access by Gopher:

chronicle.merit.edu

Select:

job openings

To access by World Wide Web:

http://chronicle.merit.edu/.ads/.links.html

Health Jobs

MedSearch America

MedSearch America is nationwide and free to the job seeker. Employers include pharmaceutical companies, sports medicine clinics, cancer treatment centers, biotech firms, HMOs, health insurance companies, laboratories, and care facilities. Jobs can be permanent, temporary, contract, or internship.

MedSearch America offers job seekers a variety of services, such as online resume posting via e-mail; resume coding to protect identity; healthcare job listings you can search by job location, category, job title, keyword, employer name, and the employer's primary industry; employer profiles; and career articles and resources.

Optional for-a-fee job seeker services include modest charges for paper resume input ($5 after first free page), optional e-mail address, and limited Internet access.

To access by World Wide Web:

http://www.medsearch.com

To access by Gopher:

gopher.medsearch.com

To access by e-mail:

office@medsearch.com

Networking with Trendies

HotWired

Wired magazine late last year opened its free Web-based online service, billing it as the Net's first "cyberstation."

It sports five main channels, one of which is a marketplace called *Coin,* which includes classified ads for jobs offered and jobs wanted.

A sampling of other attractions: *Club Wired,* 99 chat channels, and hypertexted tech news. The graphics are colorful—Newsweek mischievously labeled them "Picasso meets Egyptian hieroglyphs."

HotWired can be a meeting ground for hip designers, writers, promoters, computerites, and others who can follow its trek on the wild space. Example: Any one looking for an entry-level job in the mixed-media industry should not miss the networking ops in Hot Wired.

To access by World Wide Web:

http://www.hotwired.com/

Nursing Jobs

Nurse

This service contains job listings for nurses. Although it is maintained by the University of Warwick, in Coventry, England, it is not limited to United Kingdom jobs. Nurses with an itch to travel abroad should look in on this service.

To access by World Wide Web:

http://www.csv.warwick.ac.uk:8000/jobs.html

Technical Jobs

The Job Board

A nationwide listing of technical jobs—chiefly MIS/DP positions. New listings are added to the top of the listing file when they arrive.

To access by World Wide Web:

http://www.io.org/~jwsmith/jobs.html

NetNote

Working on the Web

Reminder: As discussed in the previous chapter, you can get on the World Wide Web—and see all the graphics and hear all the sound—by using (1) a Mosaic-like browser if you have direct Internet access (such as SLIP/PPP), or (2) using the new SlipKnot or TIA navigators if you're working with dial-up indirect access.

JOBS YOU REACH BY TELNET

The chief attraction of Telnet is that you can reach your target resource without incurring long-distance charges (assuming you have a local connection). When your choice is between Telnet or a long-distance dial-up call (using your modem), there's no contest. Three cheers for Telnet!

All Jobs, Including New Grads

Career Connection H.E.A.R.T.

This resource is free for job seekers. (Employers pay.) Most jobs are technical, but an expanding job base includes some managerial, financial, sales, and marketing positions. The company name is Heart Advertising Network, Inc.; the acronym stands for *H*uman *Re*sources *E*lectronic *A*dvertising & *R*ecruiting *T*ool. This is a menu-driven system (easy to use). You'll be asked to register and select a password so that private e-mail can be created for you. To do this, you must create a "profile," so have your resume at hand when you access this service. Remember, Telnet is the cheapest way to use this recruiter.

To access by Telnet:

    career.com

To access by modem:

    415-903-5815

Federal Jobs

FedWorld

Sometimes called the "U.S. Government Bulletin Board," FedWorld helps you see what jobs are available, but also will deliver documents, statistics, and visual materials from just about any branch of the federal government. Set up by the National Technical Information Service, FedWorld lets you reach out to more than 200 computer bulletin boards operated by the U.S. Government. Select "Federal Job Openings" from the main menu choices. You can search by agency, geographic region, or state. You can use keywords to search job openings on a local or national scope. Job announcements provide basic contract, salary, and classification information. You can download much of the information. Remember, this resource does not accept applications; you do that through the agency for which you'd like to work.

Tip: If you don't know the market rate pay for an occupation, you can get a broad hint by looking up a comparable position in the federal government.

FedWorld is also available on the World Wide Web and on Gopher.

To access:

fedworld.gov

Librarians

JobSearch Online Placement Database Service

The University of Illinois Graduate School of Library and Information Science, in Urbana-Champaign, maintains this service. Coverage is nationwide, with a heavy concentration in the Midwest, especially Illinois, and includes all levels and all library types. This outstanding job database allows you to search by library type, job type, level of experience, geographic region, pay scale, and date of availability.

NetNote

Tooling to Telnet

How do you use Telnet? Often, you just type the word telnet followed by the address. For instance, to start your research you can type:

telnet career.com

To access by Telnet:

>   alexia.lis.uiuc.edu

Login:

>   jobs

Password:

>   Urbaign

>   (Password is case sensitive)

Library Jobs

Fenner Guide Library Jobs

A "list of lists" for library jobs.

To access by Telnet:

>   gopher.lib.umich.edu

Select:

>   What's New and Featured Resources
>   Clearinghouse for Subject-Oriented Internet Resource Guides
>   All Guides
>   Library Jobs

JOBS YOU REACH BY MAILING LISTS (E-MAIL)

As explained in Chapter 3, you subscribe to listservers (and unsubscribe when you wish), and you read everything everyone says. You may wish to post your own messages.

Although most career-field listservers don't allow resume posting, they do contain news of job openings in the occupations within their focus.

Here are some examples to suggest what's available by mailing list.

FedJobs

Federal job openings, generally oriented toward current federal employees.

Send e-mail to:

   Listserv@dartcms1.dartmouth.edu

Type:

   sub fedjobs [your name]

Jobplace

An electronic discussion group for practitioners—more than 1,000 of them—in the field of career development and job search. It was started by Dr. Drema Howard, followed by Bill Felty, at the University of Kentucky. Jobplace has moved to *JobWeb* (see Chapter 1); at press time, new address details weren't set. The original address still works.

Send e-mail to:

   listserv@ukcc.uky.edu

Type:

   sub Jobplace [your name]

Young Scientists' Network
YSN

Discussions of young scientists' employment, and information on alternative careers. Lots of grant tips are given. A must-read list for the science fields.

Send e-mail to:

   ysn-joblist@atlas.chemistry.uakron.edu

Subject:

   send

Type:

   sub ysn-joblist [your name]

NetNote

Using Mailing Lists

This is general information; follow the directions given by each mailing list.

To subscribe to a specific Listserv, you usually must send an e-mail message to the mailing list provider's address. In the body of the e-mail message, type:

Subscribe [Listname Firstname Lastname]
(e.g., Subscribe Jobplace Joyce Kennedy)

Leave the subject field blank. The subscribe command causes the system to add your name to the mailing list.

To remove yourself from a mailing list, do the opposite. Use the unsub command except you need not include your name:

Unsubscribe [Listname]
(e.g., Unsubscribe Jobplace)

You can use abbreviations "sub" for subscribe, and "unsub" for unsubscribe.

The procedure is slightly different for Majordomo and other list-servers. If you don't know what to do, follow the directions above and the listserver will probably fire back a message telling you where you went wrong and how to fix it.

Careers in Information Systems
CIS-L

Information systems specialists, including professors and managers. Lots of career talk on this list.

Send e-mail to:

listserv@ube.bitnet

Subject:

new subscription

Type:

sub cis-l [your name]

Researchers in Marketing
ELMAR

As the name implies, this list is for those interested in marketing. Much of the list is academically focused.

Send e-mail to:

elmar-request@columbia.edu

Type:

sub elmar [your name]

Environmental Engineering
ENVENG-L

A list for the full spectrum of environmental engineering interests. Job postings are O.K., resumes are not.

Send e-mail to:

listserv@templevm.bitnet

Type:

sub enveng-l [your name]

International Career & Employment Network
ICEN

A listserver that contains postings of job openings all around the world, as well as postings designed to help individuals find placement abroad.

Send e-mail to:

listserv@iubvm.ucs.indiana.edu

Type:

sub ICEN-L [your name]

Volunteers in Service to America
VISTA

Available twice a month: a free copy of VISTA On-Line, an electronic bulletin featuring job opportunities from the Corporation for

National and Community Service. An electronic newsletter, not a discussion list.

Participants in VISTA (like a domestic Peace Corps) receive modest stipends, health care and, if needed, child care grants. Consider this option if you're caught in a no-experience, no-job bind. Even if you're not paid much, you will gain experience.

Send e-mail to:

listserv@american.edu

Type:

sub vista-l [your name]

5 PEOPLE Looking for Jobs

A sampling of the kinds of databases that employers and recruiters search when they're on the prowl for resumes. They may be recruiting for jobs right now . . . or window shopping for gleam-in-the-eye positions. Update your information interviewing efforts by networking on the Net.

"SPECIAL DELIVERY FOR SOO WONG LEE, MBA."

TURN YOUR PC INTO AN ALL-PURPOSE JOB INFORMATION APPLIANCE

"I got my first job out of college via the Internet using misc.resumes and worked at Hewlett Packard's graphics technology division for two years before moving to my current job," says John M. Olsen of Orem, Utah.

"After I posted my resume, a manager at HP saw it and called me to arrange a phone interview. After passing the phone interview, the company flew me out for a site visit. I had the offer before flying home," recalls Olsen, who is one of millions of people who have hooked up to their networks to trawl databases, send e-mail resumes, and interact with potential employers or with people who can lead them to employers.

Because the electronic experience is a global event, lots of resume shoppers answered my online request for their true stories. Bob Jones of the UK wrote:

"I have always found online [search] helpful with locating work, but not always in the way you might expect. About six or seven years ago I was able to reestablish contact with an old university friend, as he was on the same e-mail system here in the UK, with whom I had lost contact about seven years before. He subsequently put me in contact with a guy for whom I did some freelance work, and then I joined his company for three years.

"Last year, a friend spotted an online request which he put me on to, which resulted in a major and profitable contract."

Whether you're seeking good places to post your resume, or trying to network your way into a new job, or looking for a job in Paris, the Net appeal of taking your "show" on the road we call the information highway is hard to resist.

Here are suggestions to jump start your search.

CREATE AN OUTSTANDING ELECTRONIC RESUME

Fast growing companies across the country are using "applicant tracking systems" (job computers) to review your resumes.

In this book, we consider how to move your resume across the Internet in plain ASCII text, or in an attractive formatted version (see Chapter 7).

There's much more you should know, apart from the transportation of your resume. You should also understand how to change the *content* and *appearance* of your resume to impress job computers once it arrives in an employer's office.

Three resume tips are worth a special mention:

1. **Be sure your resume is computer-friendly**
   Resumes, increasingly, and more often than you may suspect, are sorted and ranked by the number of keywords found. Thus, the cardinal point to master is the concept of *keywords*.
      Learn to describe yourself in keywords—the terms for which employers program job computers to search. (The keywords vary, depending on the nature of the position being filled.)
      If you want to be retrieved from electronic space and considered as a candidate, you must use keywords skillfully. That's the only way a job computer can pick you out from the crowd. Resumes with the most keywords bubble to the top of the electronic heap. As long as you're not lying, load your resume with every conceivable keyword, especially those that appear frequently in the help-wanted ads that interest you.
      If your resume is not computer-friendly, take time out to make it so.

2. **Limit line size**
   Do not allow your resume text lines to exceed 65 characters (including spaces). Longer lines will not display as you intend, and may look weird.

3. **Think before you write**
   Do not include confidential information when your resume is destined for a database that will be widely searched by employers and others. You may want to eliminate the names of past employers, describing them, instead, in a generic sense: "a large manufacturer of motorized vehicles" or "a small retail establishment," for example.

For a fuller explanation of how to prepare the new style of resume, see the book I wrote with Thomas Morrow, *Electronic Resume Revolution*. You might also like to read Peter Weddle's book, *Electronic Resumes for the New Job Market*. Both books are noted in the Appendix.
    For additional advice, see Chapter 9 of this book.

MULTIMEDIA RESUMES: MOXIE OR MADNESS?

It seems like a smashing idea: the new multimedia resumes that do everything but whistle "Dixie" in their graphics, sound, text, and (sometimes) video clips. Whole graduating classes have made multimedia resumes and put them in CD-ROM "electronic resume books."

Should you jump on the multimedia minibandwagon? Unless you work in a creative field—such as art, media, multimedia, entertainment, or promotion—it's not a promising idea, for several reasons.

First, you have to make sure the recipient of your multimedia resume has the necessary equipment and the desire to play it.

The second problem involves performance. A college professor tells me he dropped the electronic resume book idea because, in their obvious discomfort at appearing before a camera, too many of the participants did not come across very well.

The clincher is that employers fear legal exposure. They are hesitant to know, prior to a hiring offer, any information that might be covered by some discrimination law—age, sex, marital status, race, and ethnic background.

PERSONALITY CAN BE POWERFUL

If you're replying to an ad, you can soften any hard-edged images a computer response may generate. Here's a charming online cover letter a reader of my newspaper column sent me. The reader identified the letter's author as a friend to whom I've given the alias of Sonja Ruiz. After the message header addressing the employer (like an inside address on a paper letter), Ruiz filled in the message subject line: "Sales Secretary position," and then delivered a message that was sure to separate her from the crowd:

Good morning!

Please ignore the attached resume.

While it does point out my extensive work experience, it does not begin to describe the intensely focused, deadline-meeting marketing environment that I just surfaced from and would like to jump back into.

You could have written the ad, "Dear Sonja:" . . . etc. A productive and intelligent professional, the strong organizational background, the sales competency, the high-energy level, and the WordPerfect 6.0—everything is exactly as ordered.

With my degree in English lit as a bonus, I am certain to be an unusually good investment for you. I'm betting you'll find me every bit as attractive a candidate as the compensation package budgeted for this position.

If you just can't wait until this evening to reach me (my preference), then you may place a discreet call to me at 123-456-7899 between 12:00 and 1:00 p.m. (my lunch hour).

Looking forward to our first meeting.

Sonja got the job.

PUT YOUR·RESUME ON INTERNET MARQUEES

"Hi Joyce, I am a professional headhunter and I work for [a major corporation], as my e-mail return address indicates.

"I regularly read the Internet resumes and have found some good leads from the process . . .[the activity] has resulted in several hires so far."

This e-mail message from Bill Wallace is representative of a dozen similar comments sent to me, suggesting that recruiters *do* window shop in the electronic malls of job seekers. To what degree? Nobody knows yet. The jury's still out on the time/effectiveness ratio of Internet resume posting.

If you're ready to "put your resume up on the Net," first review Chapter 4 for resources.

Originally, my plan was to separate job vacancy resources from resume posting resources, but, upon closer inspection, it became apparent that many resources are "working both sides of the street." The resources are difficult to separate because so many are used both to find people for jobs, and to find jobs for people.

Even so, a few destinations stand out as places to post resumes. What follows is merely a sampling; the actual listings would require a separate directory.

Employment Consultants

David Davidowicz, mentioned in Chapter 1, heads a company called *Job Finders.* He works chiefly online, but also by fax and telephone. Davidowicz is a good example of the growing legions of online employment consultants to whom you can upload your resume. For details, check by telephone: 508-840-4479; or *send e-mail to:*

> maworctr@aol.com

Online Opportunities, operated by Ward Christman, offers a regional online resume database to Philadelphia area employers. Reach the company by telephone: 610-873-2168; dial his BBS: 610-873-7170; or *send e-mail to:*

> ward.christman@jobnet.com

Professional Societies and Trade Organizations

Optolink is an example of professional and trade groups' online services, which are springing up like mushrooms in a rain forest. Check the groups that are of interest to you; telephone them and ask whether an electronic job service is available and how you join in.

Optolink is sponsored by the International Society for Optical Engineering. This World Wide Web resource focuses on the field of optics. Each month, the Optolink Employment Service runs positions-wanted ads. The ads are separated by educational level and by a category for consultants. For details, *send an e-mail message to:*

info-optolink-request@spie.org

Usenet Newsgroups

atl.resumes
> Atlanta newsgroup for resume posting.

il.jobs.resumes
> Illinois newsgroup for resume posting.

misc.jobs.misc
> Discussions about jobs and job hunting. Do not post resumes or jobs here.

misc.jobs.resumes
> Post resumes in ASCII format only.

misc.jobs.wanted
> People looking for jobs.

misc.jobs.resumes
> Universal resume posting area.

NETWORK WITH PEOPLE ON A GRAND SCALE

How do you find out about labor unions and about issues ranging from "unions, jobs, and the environment" to "women in the labor movement"? LaborNet (415-442-0220) is your answer. *To access by e-mail:*

labornet@labornet.apc.org

Career counselors and related professionals have a gabfest on Jobplace, discussed in Chapter 4. The discussion group originated at the University of Kentucky Career Center. To subscribe, *send e-mail to:*

listserv@ukcc.uky.edu

Canadians share a similar focus in a discussion group sponsored by The Canadian Association of Career Educators and Employers. Participants chat about everything from recruiting issues to job search. The discussion list is at the University of Toronto Career Centre. To subscribe, *send e-mail to:*

career@ecf.utoronto.ca

Labor unions and career issues are merely the tip of an emerald iceberg. Would you like to interact with people in the performing and visual arts? In arts-related careers, the people you know are often as important as the talent you have. Rice University's Gopher (see Chapter 4) has an arts directory that covers more than 50 Gopher sites and resources you won't want to miss.

Walter R. Ledge, a court reporter in Los Angeles, got a good job networking by proxy. He established online connections with other court reporters, one of whom did him a good turn. After hearing of a temporary opening in Los Angeles's District Court, the online pal contacted Ledge and suggested he look into the substitute job right away. Ledge jumped on the opportunity and he's been working on a day-to-day basis ever since. The best part: Ledge is in position to apply for the next permanent court reporting job opening.

What is a good way to position yourself on the Internet? Start by gaining visibility in your area of expertise. Leaders in many fields began by writing an article for a print professional journal or trade magazine. Write an article in your specialty and place it in an online discussion group library. Employers and recruiters may find your signed article and contact you.

Internships are another way to be noticed. Use the Net as an electronic King Solomon's mine for locating them. Seekers, or their advisers, go deep into cyberspace on quests for hard-to-find internships, such as "a broadcasting internship in New York City for a minority student," "an internship related to industrial psychology or human factors in Connecticut or New York City," and "an internship in Hollywood for theatrical cosmetology."

It's uncertain how may intern wannabes connect with suitable jobs, but they certainly are learning not to take "no such internships" in a print directory for an answer.

INFORMATION INTERVIEWING: WOW! LOOK AT IT NOW!

Drag it out of the pasture: The information interview is hot again. The grand old war horse of the 1970s and 1980s rides again on electronic turf.

Information interviewing originally was a technique used by individuals to ask for occupational data genuinely needed for career choices. It was not supposed to be a synonym for sneaky job interviewing. Some job seekers thought otherwise and flew under false colors. They saw information interviewing, along with networking, as the "secret of the job search." Once inside an office, they abused the generosity of employers by asking them for jobs.

After a few such experiences, businesspeople became skeptical when experienced adults asked for an information interview—"just a few minutes to explain a little about your field."

Today, critics, such as Seattle career counselor Dennis Buckmaster, say information interviewing as a job/career search technique is outmoded—"a waste of time and energy."

Buckmaster thinks he knows why people spend months on the technique and get nowhere. "Employers are on to it. They *know* it's a ruse. They *know* that when someone says, 'I'm not looking for a job, I'm only interested in your company,' that person either really wants to work there, or is so lost that he needs counseling. And it's the employer who ends up doing it."

Buckmaster expressed these beliefs in an interview with the first-rate *ReCareering Newsletter* (708-735-1980), a monthly publication originating in Lake Bluff, Illinois, for middle-years job seekers.

The Seattle career counselor and I agree on the issue. One-to-one "live" information interviews no longer have the punch they once did. Company personnel, in these lean and mean times, can't spend time on non-work-related interviews. As Buckmaster says, "They're there to solve company problems, not other people's."

That's why the opportunity to information interview on the Internet is pumping fresh energy into a proven, if shopworn, technique. People who go home from work and turn on their networked computers may be far more likely to answer questions, share information, make referrals, or even invite you in for an interview. Why? Because they're less pressured; They probably enjoy computer interaction as a hobby, and are communicating with you on their own time.

Because the electronics version is a novelty, it is likely to prove a fertile medium in which to seek information interviews. Who knows whom you might "get in to see" via computer? Until it became overwhelming, Bill Gates, one of the world's richest men, tried to answer most of his e-mail. The new information interviewing window is open, but for how long?

CAREER RESEARCH YOU CAN DO ONLINE

By Gopher and Telnet, you can reach libraries the world over, including the Library of Congress. Here is a sprinkling of other important career-related research resources.

Occupational Outlook Handbook

The *Handbook,* produced every two years by the U.S. Department of Labor, is the basic reference for descriptions of a couple of hundred of the main occupations in the economy. Almost all other occupational descriptions owe allegiance to this biannual work. It describes what workers do on the job, the training and education needed, earnings, working conditions, and expected job prospects in a wide range of occupations covering more than 100 million jobs. It provides valuable assistance to individuals who must make career decisions about their future work lives. Access is free.

To access by Gopher:

gopher://umslvma.Umsl.Edu:70/1/1/library/govdocs/ooha/oohb

NewsNet

A sophisticated electronic news clipping service, NewsNet eliminates the need to look and look for the news you need. Daily, it scans more than 17,000 newspapers and periodicals for topics of interest, then delivers the news automatically, 24 hours a day. The service is a knockout when you are preparing to interview for a particularly important position—you'll have the latest information with which to dazzle the interviewer.

You can order a customized search for your topic; the list ranges from advertising and marketing to travel and tourism. The downside is that the service is priced for companies and institutions; check with your library or university. Alternatively, you can pay an information broker to run the search for you. To obtain a reference to an information broker in your locale, call the NewsNet help desk: 800-345-1301.

Edgar

An important service of the Securities & Exchange Commission (SEC), Edgar allows free access to corporate filings with the federal government. The service is administered by New York University's Leonard J. Stern School of Business. For job seekers, this is a valuable tool for obtaining information about a company's financial status, stability, mergers, and downsizings. Edgar's readme file (orientation to the service) explains how to obtain the basic information job seekers need—corporate profiles and names of key executives—without downloading huge files. Although a large industry has grown up around the sale of financial records, you can save money by tapping into the SEC's free Edgar information system.

To access by ftp:

town.hall.org

From Edgar directory:

get readme file

TRAWLING THE GLOBAL JOB MARKET

Like a sleeping giant, the global job market is awakening. Australia's Dave Thomas (dave@softpac.com.au) says most of his global job experience focuses on technical specialists, particularly computer heavyweights:

"We are employers, as well as service/skills providers. We use the Internet and find it particularly useful and cost effective, especially when trying to locate specific skills overseas."

Short-Term Stints

The Internet is convenient to find short-term jobs as well as permanent international employment. Using online discussion groups, counselors ask and answer such queries as this:

> *Question:* "One of our clinical faculty may be in Singapore for a year. Any suggestions that I might pass on to her about finding work/working would be helpful" (from a U.S. Midwestern school of law).

> *Answer:* "Try the Internet at NUS [National University of Singapore] Singapore. The country is sufficiently labor short that the government maintains a listing of open positions for international employees" (from a counselor at another Midwestern college).

Campus career counselors routinely go online to ask for help from colleagues on advising students who want jobs in other countries, from New Zealand to South Africa, from Germany to Russia. Almost always, some suggestions come by return e-mail.

Electric Cities for Everyone

What resources can the general public use in returning from overseas employment? Several suggestions on finding a work experience abroad are given in Chapter 4, but when you're away and out of circulation for a long time, completing a round trip back to the United States can be formidable.

On Jobplace, a professional service for career counselors, a question was posed: "Any recommendations for a U.S. resident who is overseas, with a definite return date planned, who seeks a job in the U.S.?"

An answer flew back from Leo Charette, an adviser to this book:

"There is a young and growing movement—freenets, or electronic cities—on the Internet that provides free public access to individual communities."

Charette continued to say that the freenets offer splendid opportunities to electronically network from distant places. When you want to return to Cleveland or Miami or Honolulu—or approximately 100 other communities—think immediately of talking to people in the community's freenet.

Freenets are also operating in a number of countries, including Canada (Calgary, Ottawa, Montreal, Toronto, Victoria, and other cities), Germany, Italy, New Zealand, the Philippines, and Sweden, to name a few.

Acting as major job bridges over oceans, the freenets breath new life into the familiar comment, "It's a shrinking globe." To find out if there's a freenet in a particular community, you can call the National Public Telecomputing Network: 216-498-4050.

Send e-mail to:

info@nptn.org

To try out a good freenet, Telnet to CapAccess in Washington, DC:

cap.gwu.edu

Login:

guest

Password:

visitor

HOW INTERNATIONAL RESUMES DIFFER IN STYLE FROM U.S. RESUMES

An Illinois career counselor asked online recently whether resume formats are different for different countries. "Are there certain conventions that contrast with U.S. style?"

The answer is a resounding "Yes!"

The main thing for Americans to remember is that, when working overseas for a foreign employer, you are not protected by Equal Employment Opportunity laws. Your sex, race, or religion may prevent you from being hired, an abomination to freedom-loving Americans but a fact of life in some places in the world.

Check with the target country's embassy to identify preferred resume styles; specifics vary among cultures.

As an overview statement, non-U.S. employers seek longer and more detailed documents than Americans typically produce. In some cultures, they insist on knowing, up front, such non-job-related personal data as race, religion, sex, age, and occupation of parents.

My advice is to offer only job-related information no matter what they say they want.

Realists may argue that if you don't meet non-U.S. employers' demands, it's pointless to submit a resume. For instance, a resume that announces you're Jewish or female automatically will be dumped by many Middle Eastern employers. (Read: Only white, male Gentiles need apply.) "That's just the way it is," realists say. I say, "Nuts!"

The argument is an old saw, spruced up for a rerun now that the job market is becoming truly global. The realists are probably right. By refusing to cave in to blatant bias, your resume may be screened out before you can scream "foul play." Even so, I refuse to advise anyone to stuff an international resume with data certain to be used as a weapon of discrimination.

Admittedly, some employers will discriminate, no matter what, perhaps through job application forms, interviews, or private telephone calls. But why roll over and make it easy?

Let's not forget the lessons of history on a related point. A number of books specialize in resume writing for specific countries, but they're similar in philosophy to early resume books in the United States— written from the employer's view, with scant sensitivity for the job seeker.

In the 1950s, American career experts began focusing job hunters' attention on the fact that the playing field is vertical when the employer calls all the shots. The experts began suggesting highly effective coping strategies.

If you read a country-specific resume book, realize that the job seeker's needs may not best be served by "confessing" on a resume all the information many foreign employers say they want.

Talk money, for example, *after* you've been offered a job, when you can negotiate as an equal in a business deal in which you sell a portion of your life for a specific amount of compensation.

Two exceptions to the rule of *not* revealing your salary requirements are (1) when dealing with third-party recruiters, or (2) when common sense says you should establish a range of pay before flying overseas for an interview. Give yourself room to negotiate by always speaking in ranges, not in rigid dollar amounts.

The self-marketing tool we call a resume, people abroad call a curriculum vitae (CV), a Latin term meaning the course of one's life. The CV rattles on for six to eight pages, sometimes more.

Don't mistake the foreign use of the term CV with the way it is used in the United States. To Americans, a CV is an unvarnished biographical statement of education, publications, and honors earned by scholars, physicians, scientists and other high-profile achievers. The American CV does not intrude into personal areas of life.

By contrast to briefer U.S.-style resumes, the best of which are outcome-oriented and achievement-focused, not mere skeletal outlines of name, rank, and serial number—job seekers of many other nations are told to use the long-winded curriculum vitae.

"Think of a CV as a very detailed resume," advises Will Cantrell, publisher of *International Employment Hotline,* an Oakton, Virginia newsletter on overseas jobs that periodically gives CV tips.

If your CV contains fewer than six-to-eight pages, foreign recruiters may think you're hiding something, says Cantrell. If you're dealing with an American recruiter for overseas jobs, go ahead and use your American resume.

Although Cantrell advises a format in reverse chronological order, which begins with the latest info and works backward (the form most common in the United States), some international job market authorities report that the chronological-order format, which lists education and work experience from the beginning to the present, is still widely used in Europe.

Formality prevails. In Japan, for example, job hunters still fill out standard CV forms, available at Japanese book shops.

England has a suggested CV form, which is more like the American resume than not. Dr. Kate Brooks, who directs career services at Dickinson College in Carlisle, Pennsylvania, an institution with many foreign language majors who are interested in the international job market, reports that the British CV recommendation of the British Graduate Careers Advisory Services is a two-page format, and three pages for individuals with extensive experience.

For a non-English speaking country, have your CV translated into the appropriate foreign language. Send both the English and native-language versions. Use both sides of the paper, to save postage, and put your name on each sheet of paper.

NetNote

Job Search QuickList

When learning lots of new information, as you are in this book, it may be helpful to have a point of reference about the entire job search process. As we say in "onlinespeak," here's a QuickList to help you keep your bearings.

Define Yourself

- What are your interests and values?
- What are your skills?
- What is your work experience?

Identify a Work Market

- Find out about the world of work.
- Find out about jobs that use your qualifications.

Prepare Materials

- Upgrade and make computer-friendly your resumes and cover letters. Write brief versions for online job search.

Identify Employers

- Network, both one-on-one and electronically.
- Cultivate appropriate technical and executive recruiters.
- Identify appropriate third-party employment services, private and public.
- Practice using online and other electronic job search techniques to find new resources that pinpoint employers of special interest.

Practice Interviews

- Practice basic interview techniques; new computer programs can help.
- Learn about test taking; new computer programs can help.

Contact Employers

- Make the contact; learn effective telephone and online accessing techniques.
- Research the company to anticipate how your skills match a job's requirements.

Interview

- Dress correctly for the target job.
- Be on time. Be positive in your outlook.

NetNote (cont.)

- Take notes during the interview. Plan a follow-up.
- Show the right attitude. Put the employer's needs before yours; ask no self-interest questions before an offer is made.
- Make an intelligent exit: Ask for the job, or know the next action step.

Follow-Up

- Immediately evaluate your interview performance; identify what needs improvement or changing.
- Alert your references (whom you prepared in advance with a copy of your resume, highlighted with sales points).
- Write an intelligent (not cliché or rote) thank-you note.
- Telephone after five days if you haven't heard. Restate your interest.

Accept the Job

- Be clear on your job duties, mutual expectations, pay, and benefits.
- Ask for a written employment offer if you're changing jobs or relocating.

When writing your CV, Will Cantrell suggests you use the first page or two for personal information and education, followed by a career objective that identifies the position you seek, and then by pages of detailed work histories.

Personal information can include relevant facts, such as single or dual citizenship, foreign language fluency, passport number and date of expiration, previous overseas experience, security clearance, foreign travel experience, student temporary work permits, and personal interests and hobbies that suggest you'll easily adapt to an overseas environment. Unless untrue, say you have excellent health.

Work histories can be followed by a bulleted list of your accomplishments. Highlight what you achieved for your previous and present employers.

A cover letter should accompany a CV sent to any country. Often, it should be handwritten because Europeans use handwriting analysis as part of their screening.

Handwritten cover letters are common in Spain, Italy, France, and Germany, and sometimes are scrutinized by graphologists as part of the screening process. If your handwriting is iffy, enclose a typewritten version as well.

As an experienced adult dealing with recruiters, don't limit yourself as to the countries where you are willing to work. But as a student seeking a temporary job abroad, your letter should reflect a sincere desire to be in the country of your choice.

That's the long and short—international CVs and American resumes—of applying for overseas positions.

6 CyberOpportunities for Small Business

Looking for something other than a nine-to-five job? Use the Internet to land consulting stints . . . find freelance assignments . . . work from home . . . market your own business . . . move around the globe.

"THEY WANT ME IN AUSTRALIA!"

ON THE INTERNET, NOBODY KNOWS YOU'RE NOT GENERAL MOTORS

America is discovering a whole new way of working successfully without rat-racing through a commute to a Fortune 500 company.

Do you like the cartoons and illustrations in this book? Ted Goff (Kansas City), the cartoonist, and I (San Diego) have never met in the old-fashioned way: face-to-face.

When Goff read my online request for examples of people who had found work on the Internet, he faxed me the following note with samples of his work:

"I'm a professional cartoonist, and I've just started using the online services to drum up more customers for my work. We've only just bought our first computer, so I'm truly new in town.

"I suspect my use of the online services is strictly vanilla flavored at the moment, but I hope in the very near future to be doing more exciting things.

"I'm learning to use our new scanner and I plan to post examples of my cartoons on bulletin boards and ftp sites if they let me. Perhaps someday these kinds of electronic portfolios will be everywhere on the information highway.—Best regards, Ted Goff.

"P.S. Oh, by the way, could I interest you in a few cartoons for your book?"

One look at Goff's work told me he has major talent and I signed him on fast. As proof of my initial judgment, he was able to work only from a book outline, never seeing the manuscript. He did a great job!

The Internet has been an exciting tool for Goff. Through it, he has made sales in Canada and Mexico, and has received inquiries from as far away as Argentina and Austria. Among the imaginative techniques he uses to find potential customers is a posting of his "invisible cartoons" to Usenet newsgroups.

Most newsgroups exchange only text messages, so Goff sends a short teaser to describe each cartoon. In parentheses, he asks the reader to "Close your eyes and visualize a beautiful drawing of this gag. That's it! Perfect!"

This highly skilled artist's invisible cartoons always contain a "signature" block—four or five lines describing how to contact him.

Goff says that, to him, the Internet and online services have become essential for working at home. Not only have they multiplied the size of his marketplace, but they keep him in constant contact with many other cartoonists, editors, and writers. Thanks to the electronic dimension, "They've become my coworkers," he says.

One more reason Goff loves to use the Internet: "Now I can get mail on Sunday."

NO MYSTERY ABOUT THIS ONLINE SUCCESS STORY

How can you earn $100,000+ and live in paradise? A Canadian private eye made it all come true by using the Internet. Let's walk through some of the case files of Banner Investigations.

The Case of the $50 Million Fraud

Licensed Private Investigator: Banner Investigations

Client: A law firm in New Zealand

> **Assignment:** To conduct a background investigation on two Canadian men doing business as an interglobal banking corporation. The deal involved a business transaction of $50 million between a Hong Kong corporation and a Canadian bank. The Canadians identified for investigation were set to collect a security deposit of $5 million for negotiating the deal. The New Zealand law firm, acting on behalf of its Hong Kong client, needed verification of legitimacy.

> **Results:** Just 35 hours after transmitting its request electronically, the client had documents, court evidence, and other information showing the two Canadians had been involved in fraud and theft scams eerily similar to the offer involving the New Zealand law firm's clients. Both men were awaiting trial on other charges at the time of the investigation.

The Case of the Prisoner-Promoter

Licensed Private Investigator: Banner Investigations

Client: Potential real estate buyer, located in Asia

> **Assignment**: Investigate a real estate promoter offering a wide choice of properties, in locations from Canada to Asia, at bargain prices. The Asian client was suspicious because the promoter's track record was unknown.

> **Results:** More than 44 pages of documented evidence supported the client's suspicion of fraud. The investigator also discovered that the promoter was hawking offerings from a jail cell! The felon, already convicted of fraudulent business practices, was serving an 18-month sentence under house arrest, using a court-ordered electronic monitoring system.

The Case of the Confident Crook

Licensed Private Investigator: Banner Investigations

Client: A business partnership

> **Assignment**: A former member of the client partnership had stolen $2 million and fled the United States. The ex-partner, already gone

for a year, was believed to be residing in Canada, but earlier attempts to find him had been unsuccessful.

Results: In fewer than 18 hours, the fugitive was located, his business identified, and his assets attached. The suspect had been so certain his former partners would be unable to find him that he had made no attempt to hide his wealth.

Barrie E.R. Adkins, a licensed private investigator in Canada, handled all of these cases from his home base in the beautiful city of Victoria, British Columbia.

Along with years of training and experience as an investigator, Adkins is a computer specialist—skilled in using e-mail, networks, databases, public records, and other cyberspace resources in his successful agency, Banner Investigations.

Adkins understands that contemporary sleuthing requires contemporary marketing. He proved he was on target by going online as soon as he opened his company.

Word spread of his ability to use computers to keep people from becoming victims of scam artists. The PI continues to monitor bulletin boards, prospecting for business leads. He has turned a number of postings into business opportunities. When he finds a request that could benefit from his expertise, he follows up with a letter asking if the problem has been solved. When it looks as though he has generated a business lead, Adkins sends press clippings about his company's successes, and suggests that he may be able to solve the problem.

Adkins reaps more than $100,000 a year from Banner Investigations, and the business continues to grow.

Because Adkins understood early that nerd is nice, and geek is chic, he has claimed the prize that many of us long for: a six-figure income from working on our own terms.

INFORMATION AGE MEETS MAIN STREET

America's 15 million small businesses are becoming as likely to bring in computers and digitized ways of doing business as their bigger counterparts. Most now realize they must automate or die.

Two reasons the mom-and-pops are exploiting technology are: (1) their sons and daughters learned how to use computers in college and are now in the business, and (2) a wave of corporate expatriates have voluntarily or involuntarily decided life is better on the small side.

According to *Business Week* (November 21, 1994): "Small businesses are entering the information age with the same zeal Corporate America did a decade ago."

There's a rippling effect, too, says Business Week. "As big companies have downsized and eliminated departments, they have farmed out more and more work."

Corporate restructuring and easier, cheaper technology have massive implications for people who no longer wish to be nine-to-fivers.

For people who want to work at home and who are willing to lose their technological virginity, the Net can be the answer to prayers.

Small business opportunities grow ripe in nearly every industry, in every nook and hamlet. As the Internet moves into public awareness, it is not hype to say that it will fundamentally open new ways of doing business.

Larry Grant, who with his mother, Olivia Grant, manages Grant's Flowers and Greenhouses in Ann Arbor, Michigan, says the firm went on the Net last year and, within a few months, began getting almost as many orders from the Net as from private floral networks.

ADVENTURE WRITER FINDS WORK ON INTERNET

Meet a man who gets paid to do full-time what half the men in America dream of doing on weekends: Gary P. Joyce (garyj@li.net) of Holbrook, New York.

Joyce had been using the CompuServe service for about two years, and the Internet for one month, when we connected online.

If an activity is adventuresome, fun, and can be done outdoors, Joyce is interested.

Whether it's caving, hang gliding, white water rafting, paragliding, surfing, ice climbing, rock climbing, surf kayaking, scuba diving, mountain biking, or windsurfing—Joyce does it, writes about it, and photographs it. The riskier the assignment, the more Joyce relishes the work.

Joyce earns a full-time living doing what he loves. He splits sales fairly evenly between well-known general audience publications and sport-specific magazines.

Here's how he's harvesting writing assignments from the electronic fields:

"After getting into cyberspace, the first major event that affected my career was an opportunity to return to Vietnam as a journalist. I'd done three combat tours there during the war and had returned in 1993.

"Online, I met the leader of a group of Detroit physicians who had been invited by the Vietnamese government to assess their country's health care system. I asked the physician if he had an open slot—a month later I was in Hanoi."

Gary's first sale as a result of that trip was of photography to a Canadian CD-ROM producer, whom he also met online. The trip also resulted in *Teepee Man,* an ongoing project of essays about the war and its aftermath that has already been received with interest by an agent Joyce met online.

Sometimes the online contact is step one; step two is when the new professional acquaintances come through with job leads, as Joyce's beach experience illustrates.

"After seeing an e-mail query about beach erosion, I started 'talking' with the sender, who turned out to be the president of a Nova Scotia documentary production company. The project was a story on beach erosion, something I'm pretty familiar with. I had the camera crew stay at my home when they filmed on the Long Island beaches, and got them into some recently destroyed coastal areas. They returned the favor when I pulled in three magazine assignments that they'd tipped me to in their neck of the woods—stories on surfing, diving, and rafting."

Joyce considers the Internet to be a kind of Electronic Opportunity Knocking medium, and he listens with both ears.

"I've got a video and a radio script out to production companies I met on the Internet. Because of my outdoor adventure specialty, my name has gotten around now and I'm getting lots of online inquiries as to whether I can provide this, that, or the other thing. Smart magazine editors already know that using the Internet in the assignment process can result in incredibly fast turnaround times."

Joyce has learned to use the Net for researching the background for his work.

"I recently used both CompuServe and the Internet for a piece I was writing on wetsuits and drysuits. All the interviews and opinions in the article were taken from queries I sent out online to a variety of places where those reading would use the suits."

Joyce has used the online medium to help other creative people, as well as himself.

"I've recommended three other writers I've met online to *New York Outdoors,* a magazine for which I am a consulting editor."

What else does the Internet offer freelance writers, other than paid assignments? Gary Joyce's take on that question may surprise you.

"I've grabbed about 15 assignments off the wires, any one of which has more than paid for the money spent on online costs over the past two years. Among the things I've done online: I've purchased a bargain motor drive for a camera, met a rock climbing partner and a paddling partner, and stayed current on what's going on in a variety of my adventure specialties.

"All these connections allow me to avoid that peculiar alienation that comes with freelancing and the lack of outside input. Writing is a solitary, lonely occupation, but it'd be a damn sight lonelier without the communications afforded me by my trusty ol' computer. You can't exactly explain writing as a job to a nine-to-fiver and expect any kind of understanding. They just think you're always having fun—although, admittedly, I do keep my fun quotient up! Still, it gets lonely in my home office."

INTERNET: A NEW HOME BASE FOR WRITERS AND EDITORS

Writers and editors get jobs through the Internet even when surfing in cyberspace is not recognized as a ride toward employment.

Lisa M. Balbes, PhD, a consultant and freelance writer in Columbus, Ohio (balbes@osiris.rti.org), does quality assessments of scientific software. An executive editor for a technical publication recently noticed her message commenting on an issue in a non-related newsgroup, and contacted Balbes. She was hired to edit scientific documents. The job has turned into an ongoing assignment paying moderate but steady fees.

David Farkas (CompuServe 73150,3143) agrees that the online medium is a happy hunting ground for people whose creative skills can be used in many ways. A freelance illustrator and writer in Amherst, Massachusetts, Farkas was initiated into the dreaded laid-off club after six years as a marketing representative and communications development specialist for an energy conservation consulting firm.

Saying to himself, "I'm a talented guy, I can do better on my own," Farkas turned his second-income business, The Light Works!, into a full-time venture, marketing his services online. He finds that more work opportunities develop online than through the pipeline of trade publications.

Farkas subscribes to advice I heard again and again while researching this book: "Start a conversation online with someone, find a common ground, and go on from there."

Optimistic about what the electronic dimension holds for tomorrow, Farkas speculates: "My guess is that, in writing, online will be one of the main ways people will network and find freelance work."

Thousands of writers, artists, editors, and news producers everywhere meet and mingle on the *CompuServe JForum*. Within *JForum* are bountiful options, including *NASW Online,* a focus for the National Association of Science Writers.

The relevant *JForum* option for most journalism job hunters is *Jobs and Stringers,* a place to look for—or to post—jobs in print, broadcast, and online media. Some jobs in this forum are full-time permanent; others are part-time, or one-shot assignments.

RECRUITERS FIND INTERNET RIGHT ON THE MONEY

"Recruiters around the world have found their way to the Internet," says Bill Vick, an executive recruiter and president of Vick and Associates in Plano, Texas.

Writing in *Employment Marketplace* (Spring, 1995), a leading professional publication for employment professionals (P.O. Box 31112, St. Louis, Missouri 63131), Vick says the online market is set to explode, with vast implications for technical and executive recruiters.

"It's awesome how the Net is being used to boost revenues by recruiters around the world as they post searches and find candidates. More than 2,000 postings are made daily because it works." Based on growth rates, Vick expects more than 10,000 postings daily within a year or two.

"Recruiters are finding and placing candidates because of the Internet. Although the majority of people using Internet today are technically inclined, that is changing. Mainstream America is ready to join up and sign on," Vick believes.

What's all the excitement about the Net? Vick sees an employment revolution in the making.

"When customers have the ability to deal directly with a manufacturer and save time and money in the process, the middle agents have to change the way they do business—or change businesses. It's like what happened to small-town America when box stores like Walmart appeared on the scene.

"Let's not forget that we, the recruiters, are, in fact, the middle agents between the client and the candidate. Rather than allow the Internet to put us out of business, let's use it to put us in a different kind of business. I mean a business where e-mail replaces a fax, where electronic posting replaces blind sourcing or supplements advertising, and where technology increases our span of control so we are able to do more things more effectively," says Vick.

Vick is passionate in his fervor; he understands that the stakes are huge. A $7 billion recruiting industry is facing the most serious challenge to its status quo in its three-decade history.

One of Vick's answers is the *Recruiters OnLine Network.* The Network produces the *Recruiter News Digest,* a mailing list that serves as a clearinghouse for recruiters to share business and ideas. A World Wide Web site was being established at press time.

This free online forum is set up exclusively for the permanent and temporary employment industries. Because it is moderated (watched over) by Vick, the general public cannot dial in and read the jobs posted. (Resumes are not posted.) Within the first couple of weeks after the Digest went online late last year, more than 250 recruiting firms signed up; now more than 1,000 have subscribed.

To give you some of the flavor of the interactions, here are several excerpts from The Recruiter News Digest:

> *Does that [list of stringent candidate specifications] sound too rigid? Orders from Headquarters, folks! My client is extremely picky. Of the last 250 candidates I sent these people, 78 percent were rejected out of hand. Of the remaining candidates, 93 percent weren't even given a first interview. Of the remaining, only two candidates were interviewed more than once, and only one of those was offered a position. It was a very handsome position, indeed, but it took four and a half months! If you have the right candidates, I will split some of the fee with you.*

> *I'm looking for help on this SF [San Francisco] position. Must be recognized industry superstar. Compensation in the $140 [thousand] range. Fee is flat $16,000. Will split 50/50.*

> *I am a human resources consultant on assignment to a client in Rhode Island. Since they are paying me to do candidate development, I figured I would put this out to see if anyone is interested in assisting me with this project, or if anyone knows of a good research organization that specializes in sales.*

Recruiting professionals can only subscribe by contacting Bill Vick. To contact by telephone outside prime time: 214-612-8425 or *send e-mail to:* vick@onramp.net).

MILES-APART ASSOCIATES IN ONLINE RESUME BUSINESS

"With my laptop, fax modem, and cellular telephone, I'm ready to continue my explorations of computer pathways along America's byways," says Debarah H. Wilson. Her motto: "Have talent, will travel." A year ago she did exactly that, relocating from Menlo Park, California to Austin, Texas, where she is a career consultant at Professional Career Consultants (CareerPro2 @aol.com).

Across the nation in Morrisonville, New York, Wayne Gonyea (CareerPro1@aol.com) took an early retirement, after 33 years with the State of New York, to concentrate on his new business, OnLine Solutions, Inc. (See Chapter 7.) "With the Internet, the whole globe is a new kind of marketplace for people to find jobs," Gonyea says.

Until recently, Gonyea and Wilson had never met face-to-face. No matter. These days, what's a couple of thousand miles between business associates who know how to click their way around the globe? When the Internet enters the picture, distant locations are no longer an obstacle in doing business together.

How did the Gonyea-Wilson matchup happen? Wilson responded to an advertisement for a representative to supply job listings and resumes to Help-Wanted USA, a company that can be accessed online in a number of ways. (See Chapter 4.)

When Gonyea followed up the response with a telephone call, he found that Wilson is expert at writing keyword resumes. (See Chapter 5.) Immediately, they began to collaborate on writing features for career publications about the new ways to job hunt. Their talents mesh in other professional ways as well.

Gonyea's company, OnLine Solutions, charges an annual subscription fee. Its services include putting resumes online where employers can view them. For a small additional fee, Gonyea will post a confidential resume. Among places where Gonyea's company posts resumes are the Internet's Online Career Center, and America Online's Career Center (similar names, separate entities).

Where does Wilson enter into the picture? If an employer is using a job computer and the computer can't "read" your resume, you'll be electronically screened out. Keywords are vital in helping job computers pull your resume out of a database. Not too many people know how to construct keyword resumes yet. That's why, as an optional service, Wilson will rewrite a resume for a subscriber to OnLine Solutions.

On a full-time basis, the business is only a year old, but Wayne Gonyea already has received resumes from such places as Canada, the United Kingdom, Saudi Arabia, and Trinidad, as well as Cupertino, California, Austin, Texas, Pompano Beach, Florida, and Long Island, New York.

And while the domestic business is increasing, many of OnLine Solutions' employment connections thus far are in the international marketplace.

In the jargon of today's business, the new Gonyea-Wilson strategic alliance has produced dividends for both parties: A referral chain has evolved as one client leads to another. As a result, both associates now have busy professional calendars.

One of the dividends is off the business books. Having met online, Gonyea and Wilson, both unmarried, have developed a social relationship.

CONSULTANTS AND CONTRACTORS: MARKET YOUR SERVICES ONLINE

Jeff Porten (jeffporten@aol.com) is a liberal arts major who graduated from the University of Pennsylvania and now lives in Washington, DC, earning his living as a Macintosh and Internet consultant. Porten prospects for clients on the Net, partly by checking in with Internet-related mailing list discussion groups; when the subject turns to a technical problem, Porten is on the spot, available to be engaged as a consultant. The Internet is a great resource for him professionally, he says.

"When a client calls with a question I can't answer, I spend a couple of hours browsing on the Net and can become an instant expert on the problem," Porten says.

A point the consultant emphasizes is that people count on the Internet: "It's not the online resources per se, meaning the static documents, that are valuable, so much as the human connections—being able to reach people who can help with your work. The Net is useful more for the thousands of experts it connects me to than for any document it provides."

Porten is in the first wave of professionals who are chiefly technical troops, seeking contracts and consulting jobs. Reinforcements are definitely on the way. Advertising executives, travel agents, merchants, and defense contractors, for instance, are discovering what the Internet can do for them.

Rickard Associates, an editorial company that produces magazines and marketing materials, is headquartered in an old house in Hopewell, New Jersey. The owner, Wendy Rickard, hires an art director in Arizona, editors in Florida and Michigan, and freelancers from all over. At this typical virtual company, the only people showing up for work each day at the company office are Wendy and her assistant. (If you wish to contact Rickard, please do so only by e-mail: wrickard@aol.com; no telephone inquiries, please.)

SELECTED RESOURCES FOR SMALL BUSINESS

Here are a few key resources to show you the way to the treasury when you start using the Internet to make business trips.

Internet Business Advantage

This monthly publication is outstanding in showing how small companies can compete head-to-head with big companies—and win. It isn't for Internet freshmen, but sophomores will find it very understandable. Published by Wentworth Worldwide Media, *Internet Business Advantage* is a hands-on, here's-how-you-do-it reporting of what is really new. (See the Appendix.)

Wildcat!

A popularity runaway, this software from Mustang Software Inc. (see Chapter 8) makes it a snap for a business to set up its own bulletin board. The business suite program, which sells for less than $1,000, allows customers and employees to easily communicate with each other. With a bulletin board, you can fill orders, handle service inquiries, give price quotes, and more.

In Boston, the law firm of Hale & Dorr keeps its BBS humming to cut the costs of routine work. As an illustration, when a client company needs a contract for a foreign distributor, it can fill out an electronic questionnaire and zip it over the Internet to one of the law firm's computers. Expert systems software drafts the contract from boilerplate text, a lawyer fixes blips, and the document goes back over the Net to the client, along with a list of recommended lawyers in the distributor's country.

NetworkMCI Business

Check out the nation's first single-source package to contain e-mail and fax messaging, information services with automated news monitoring, document sharing and videoconferencing, online multimedia business catalogs, and access to the Internet. A Windows-based package, networkMCI business is for all sizes of businesses. Call a local MCI service number, or use the MCI fax reply system: Call 800-289-7112, and follow the voice prompts.

MouseTracks

This World Wide Web resource of New South Network Services offers marketing help—a priority for most small businesses. Looking at this Web page does not mean you intend to put your business on the Web. It is simply a means of getting such information as *The New Medium* (a list of those using the Internet to transcend paper) and *The List of Marketing Lists* (an enumeration of the e-mail lists that exist) to discuss marketing.

In anticipation of handsome profits or status, some 2,000 companies (up from 300 a year ago) are already Webbed. This is explosive growth. If you hope to put up a storefront on the Web, you may want to access the *Hall of Malls,* which identifies a group of electronic storefronts, and *Nuts and Bolts,* which covers technical topics useful in "capturing clicks" (getting customers to click on your wares).

To access by World Wide Web:

   http://nsns.com/MouseTracks/

Charm Net Home Page

This commercial Web service offers a way to advertise your services on the Net, as well as a long list of topics of interest to entrepreneurs: economic data, stock quotes, information from collegiate schools of business, and the Internet Better Business Bureau.

To access by World Wide Web:

> http://www.charm.net/~web/Vlib/Misc/Jobs.html

Bizopps Connection

This commercial BBS, located in Los Angeles and operated by Success Ventures Enterprises, Inc., is designed for individuals interested in buying a business or franchise, seeking venture capital sources, or looking for opportunity seekers or money making opportunities. You can use this BBS free to check out samples of its content, but you'll have to pay for full access.

> Modem: 310-677-7034.

CompuServe's Working from Home Forum

This resource (see Chapter 4) has sections on scaring up business, running a business, consulting, tax help, and legal matters, to name just a few of the attractions.

Delphi's Business Forum

More than a dozen separate small business specialty areas are offered, from public relations to home business. (See Chapter 4.)

Prodigy's International Business BBS

A magnet for those doing business across the border, this Prodigy BBS offers a wide list of topics on doing business in other countries. (See Chapter 4.)

SBA-Online

The Small Business Administration's BBS is loaded with information. Entrepreneurs will find more than 26 occupational areas (including information science and librarianship), a huge library of text files to download, and information on the SBA's personal business counseling. No job openings are listed.

Virtual Company Hires Trainers by Internet

From: Marshall P. Cline, PhD, President, Paradigm Shift, Inc., Norwood, NY

To: Joyce Lain Kennedy, Sun Features, Inc., Carlsbad, CA

In answer to your request for experiences of virtual companies, we rely heavily on the Internet for our business operations. We provide training and consulting in object-oriented programming languages and techniques.

We currently have five trainer/consultants. Each lives in a different state: Missouri, New York, North Carolina, Texas, and Virginia. Each travels to our customer sites on a weekly basis (our customers currently are throughout the United States, Canada, and Mexico). Each trainer travels 30 weeks a year minimum, and works on projects at home the remainder of the year.

We have grown from two to seven employees in the past two years. One main source of finding PhD-level trainers is posting in misc.jobs.offered [newsgroup].

We have received hundreds of qualified resumes this way. We communicate with those we do not hire and have worked out contractual arrangements with some.

We communicate daily via e-mail on the Internet, passing course materials back and forth. We also maintain the Frequently Asked Questions list on comp.lang.c++.

Twice a year we have a company get-together—at Christmas and on July 4. This is the only face-to-face contact we have with all our employees at one time.

We appreciate the Internet.

To access by World Wide Web:

> http://www.sbaonline.sba.gov

To access by Gopher:

> gopher://www.sbaonline.sba.gov

To access (limited) by modem:

> 800-697-4636

For more information, call the SBA Technical Support line at 202-205-6400.

You Can Meet Business Partners around the World

Want to expand your reach and do small business in other countries? Below is an example of the kinds of contacts you can make on the Internet. (Please note that no endorsement is made of Mr. Gnidenko's offer—the example is for illustrative purposes only.)

Date: Sat, 29 Oct 94 13:46:55 +0400 (MSD)
From: "Vadim V. Gnidenko" < kivi@kivi.saratov.su >
To: jlk@sunfeatures.com
Subject: Re: [NEWS] TO: System Head (Moderator, Sysop, List Owner, Group Veteran

Dear Mr. Kennedy:
For your book I can give the following information:
email:kivi@kivi.saratov.su.
Location: Saratov, Russia
Firm: KIVI-K&V ltd
Name: Vadim
Surname:Gnidenko
The owner of small business.
We specialize: international trade promotion, business-information services, export labour resource from Russia.
We seeking partners in other country for collaboration.
Mine system: IBM PC/AT-486, Demos Mail. Ver. 1.14a
Please let me know about Your book, as finish.
Best regards,
Vadim Gnidenko
president of K&V ltd, Saratov,Russia

```
 (*)        Business-information service firm     K&V ltd
 / \—\      of .34, home 10, proezd Kotovskogo-street
   \/ \     Saratov, 410002, Russia
   _T_      phone/fax: +7-845-226-3090
            fax: +7-095-531-2403 KIVI
```

GEnie's Small Business RoundTables

The discussion groups that GEnie calls RoundTables can be invaluable to small businesspeople. (See Chapter 4.) With sections on starting a business, finding customers, tips on sales and advertising, running a business, and home office computing issues, the RoundTables have particular appeal to the self-employed and the entrepreneur.

On the Books

Need a crash course on how to bait the cyberhook? Read *The Internet Business Book* by Jill H. Ellsworth and Matthew V. Ellsworth. (See the Appendix.) You'll learn how to get in on the ground floor of doing business on the Net.

7 Where Do I Start? (And Where's the Panic Button?)

Are you ready to make the right connections? Here are answers to basic questions, and a few special technical tips to readers who are playing the job market. Remember, when in doubt, log out.

"YOU FORGOT TO INSTALL THE HYSTERIA SUPPRESSOR."

COMMONLY ASKED "HOOK UP" QUESTIONS

When I mentioned the idea of job hunting by computer, my friends and acquaintances thought it sounded fascinating. They asked lots of questions, but several are evergreens and are answered here.

What Equipment Do I Need to Get on the Infohighway?

The basic requirements for an individual are: a personal computer, a modem, a communications program, access to a telephone line, and an account with an Internet service provider.

What If I Don't Have a Computer?

You can use or rent a computer from these sources: friends, copy shops, libraries, high schools, colleges and universities, community agencies, and computer rental firms.

If you have a friend who knows computer market values, you can pick up computer bargains at swap meets and through newspaper ads. Be aware that computer sellers may think their hardware is worth more than it is. Prices are dropping on new computers; a lot of older computers are now surplus.

Must the Computer Be a Muscle Machine?

No. The computer need not be state of the art, although the ability to use a Macintosh computer or Microsoft Windows on an IBM-compatible PC is a help. Windows software isn't absolutely necessary—Dos with the appropriate communications software works, but Dos is moving to the back burner as new programs are introduced.

What Is a Modem?

A modem is the piece of electronic equipment that allows your computer to communicate with other computers through the telephone lines. It is the "black box" that lets your computer kiss up to another computer. The first generation of modems crawled, by today's lightning standards. Your modem should have a speed of at least 14,400 bits per second (bps), and 28,800 bps is preferable. A 14,400-bps modem is fine for retrieving text,

Top 10 Tips for Buying PCs

Computer coach Michael Erbschole of American Business Network, in Encinitas, California, offers these suggestions to would-be-purchasers of an IBM-compatible personal computer:

1. Be careful of package deals that are made to look like bargains. The least expensive package may require further investment, in the very near future.

2. Make sure your new PC has sufficient storage. PCs with less than 500 megabytes of hard-disk space will be rapidly overtaken by new software, which requires more storage space with every release.

3. Make sure your new PC has sufficient memory. PCs with less than 4 megabytes of RAM (random access memory) often have difficulty running current releases of software. Many packages run better with at least 8 megabytes of memory.

4. Buy a PC to which you can easily add more memory in the future. Make sure that you can upgrade and increase your memory with off-the-shelf chips. If you buy a PC that requires the use of manufacturers' memory chips, you will likely pay more for upgrading your RAM.

5. Buy a PC with built-in modem. This will save time and money, compared to adding a modem later. Unless you have the skill and knowledge to install these add-on devices, it may prove more complicated than you expect.

6. Buy a PC capable of reading both 3.5-inch and 5.25-inch floppy disks. Although most new software is being delivered on 3.5-inch floppy disks or CD-ROMs, having a 5.25-inch floppy drive will allow more flexibility in moving electronic files and databases from older PCs that often had only 5.25-inch floppy drives.

7. Buy a PC with a CD-ROM already installed, to avoid future installation costs and hassles, and to take advantage of many new software products that require CD-ROM drives.

8. Carefully choose your monitor. Low cost packages usually come with poor 14-inch monitors, which can cause considerable eye strain. You will benefit from a better and larger monitor.

9. Buy a PC that uses a standard 101 keyboard; avoid strangely configured keyboards. The standard 101 keyboard allows for easy replacement.

10. Make sure you get manuals and diskettes for the software preloaded into your computer by retailers.

NetNote (cont.)

Tips for Buying Macs

San Mateo (California)-based Tom Wills, an adviser to this book, is a Macintosh computer fan. Wills says that if you're thinking about buying a Mac computer, the list of things to look for is almost exactly the same as the list for a PC (above). The exceptions are: internal modems are not necessarily better (item 5 above) and all Macs use 3.5-inch disks (item 6 above).

Which type of computer is best for you? I asked Seattle computer guru John Hedtke that question. Hedtke uses an IBM-compatible PC, but his wife, Patricia, is a Mac person. "We have a mixed marriage," Hedtke jokes.

---

but using one to bring into your computer the immense graphical files at many World Wide Web sites is like trying to fill a swimming pool with a garden hose.

Do I Need a Separate Telephone Line for My Modem?

It's much more convenient to have a separate dedicated line for your computer, but it isn't essential. You can use the same line for voice telephone calls and modem transmissions, if you must.

Why Do I Need Communications Software?

To use your modem, you need special communications software, such as Crosstalk, HyperAccess, Procomm, QmodemPro, Smartcom II, or Wincom. Otherwise, the modem just sits there like a telephone off the hook. Most modem packages are bundled with communications software.

Almost all leading programs feature an automated dialing directory and the ability to upload and download files. These features allow you to dial up any number of online services and BBSes, an advantage if you plan to do shotgun resume distribution.

How Do I Hook Up to an Online Service?

Read the literature for each service and determine which one best fits your requirements.

If, after reading the literature or taking advantage of a free trial period, you're still puzzled, contact a local computer club or users' group for advice. You can find these groups by asking at computer retail stores. Club members usually staff booths at local computer fairs.

In San Diego, for instance, the largest computer club has many members who, during an active-duty hitch, once taught in U.S. Navy computer schools. These retired Navy teachers are walking encyclopedias of computer know-how and, in my experience, are glad to help newbies figure out how to get started.

If you can't locate a computer club locally for free informal or paid tutorial help, consider a continuing education course in computers at a nearby high school at night, a course at a community college or university, or a brief workshop at a proprietary program, such as The Learning Annex or New Horizons.

High school teachers and college instructors may be able to recommend student tutors who, for a moderate hourly fee, will come to your home and teach you how to hug your computer and send it out to scout for a job.

It wouldn't hurt to read a couple of Internet guides in advance. (See the Appendix for a selection.) Your next step is to decide which kind of Internet connection you want.

How Do I Hook Up to the Internet?

You can use the Internet through *direct access* or *indirect access.*

Direct access is comprehensive; you have more freedom to go where you want and do what you want.

Indirect access is more common. Your computer is an extension of a main computer, usually connected by a modem. The owner of the main computer may decide where you can go and what you can do. One drawback: When you download files, you must download them twice—once to the host computer and then to your computer.

Direct or indirect, the routes go by different names, and there are variations of each. Here are the most common.

Permanent Connection: Easy as 1-2-3

A direct connection, such as a T-1 line, which costs thousands of dollars per year, is what some institutions and sizable companies have. The connection is theirs alone, and unauthorized individuals cannot use it. The direct route offers a full sweep of the Net, like an around-the-world tour. It's somewhat like having a TV satellite dish that permits you to bring in a zillion stations.

Suppose you attend a college, or work for a company, organization, or other entity that has a direct, permanent connection. If you can use it, you've got a sweet deal. Not only do you probably not have to pay, but getting on and off the Internet is a breeze. You just sit at one of your organization's terminals or computers, and enter the commands that have been provided to you by the system administrator. Lucky you.

Dial-in Shell Accounts: A Tad More Difficult

These are also called dial-in accounts and using one is not difficult if someone gives you a cheatsheet or if you have a technical brain in your head. Otherwise, ask your Internet service provider for a cheatsheet to use until you get the hang of it.

If you're a total neophyte, pester an experienced user or hire a computer coach to start you off. As an alternative, read either the light and bright *The Complete idiot's Guide to the Internet* by Peter Kent, or, for industrial-strength help, read *Internet Guide for New Users* by Daniel Dern (both are listed in the Appendix).

Dial-in Direct Connection: Harder by Half

The most familiar types of this connection are SLIP and PPP accounts. (See the Glossary.) Using a SLIP or PPP connection is more complicated than using a dial-in shell account. In a nutshell, this is a shared route to the Internet. You get the same access but you're sharing the ride. You can gain full benefits, such as copying files directly to and from your computer's hard drive. Depending on your software, you may be able to do several things at once. Unless you're technically minded, don't start out with this type of connection.

Tip: To avoid long-distance charges, get an Internet service provider that offers a local telephone number.

Starting with a user-friendly commercial online service, such as America Online or CompuServe, may be the best way to break the Internet ice.

RESUME POSTING BASICS

After you've prepared your computer-friendly resume, you'll have some questions about the steps.

How Does the E-Mail Addressing System Work?

E-mail addresses are not case-sensitive. That is, you usually can use all lowercase letters, which is the standard style. But if you use all capital letters, it won't matter one way or the other.

E-mail addresses may look like gibberish until you can recognize the elements and their order of appearance. Before getting to the details, remember that Internet uses a *domain name system,* which is how computers contact each other with messages.

In a domain name system, a local computer goes through a series of contacts (based on numbers; each computer has a number) until it reaches the computer (the *domain*) that collects mail for the person you wish to reach. The parts of a domain name are similar to a zip code, a street, and the specific building on that street. Each part of a domain is called a *sub-domain.* The *top-level domain* is the most general specification.

In understanding e-mail addresses, remember that your address is in two parts: your user ID name, and your *domain* name; each is separated by an @ sign. The text to the left of the sign is your user ID name, to the right your domain name.

Let's look at hypothetical Margaret Kline's e-mail address— *mkline@ajax.com*—as an example. Her login name *(mkline)* is followed by the "at" sign (@). After that comes the first part of her domain name—her location, which, in this case, is the name of her company *(ajax),* followed by a dot and the top-level domain indicating it is a commercial site *(.com).*

To clarify, the first part of the address, the part before the @ sign is a person's unique user identification, or user ID. A user ID name can be simple, like Margaret's, or it can be any combination of letters and numbers, including a dash or period.

The information right after the @ sign indicates a person's location, which may be the name of a company, or other entity. Sometimes it's the name of a commercial Internet service provider. For example, if Margaret obtained Internet access through a commercial service provider, Margaret's address might be *mkline@prodigy.com.* (The online information service Prodigy is serving as the Internet service provider.)

The next item in the address, the top-level in the domain name system, suggests what kind of place it is.

There are a number of different types of top-level domains, each with a different three-letter ending. Here are the ones most commonly used.

.com commercial

.edu educational

.gov governmental

.int international

.mil military

.net network

.org nonprofit organization

Not commonly employed for sites within the United States, the last two letters of a domain name may indicate the country location. For instance, if you see *preisendorfer@gold.com.de,* the *.de* tells you the address is in Germany. If there is no two-letter country extension to a domain address, assume it's located in the United States. Here are selected international domain extension codes:

.au	Australia
.ca	Canada
.ch	Switzerland
.de	Germany
.dk	Denmark
.es	Spain
.fi	Finland
.fr	France
.ie	Ireland
.il	Israel
.in	India
.it	Italy
.jp	Japan
.mx	Mexico
.nl	Netherlands
.no	Norway
.nz	New Zealand
.pl	Poland
.ru	Russia
.se	Sweden
.uk	United Kingdom
.us	United States

To be certain any e-mail you send over the Net gets there in one piece, or at all, you must have the recipient's exact, precise, individual e-mail address. New style white page directories, such as Aldea Publishing Company's *NetPages,* contain e-mail addresses.

You also can use Internet online search tools such as *Finger* (see the Glossary) to find your intended.

Calling to confirm an address is strongly recommended when you are seriously interested in a particular prospective employer and are not dead certain about the e-mail address. Just ask whoever answers the telephone: "Can you please give me [Joe Big-shot's] e-mail address?"

Every e-mail message has several main parts:

- *A header* (the recipient's e-mail address, and the sender's e-mail address); note: Your computer should be set up so that your e-mail address automatically appears on each message;
- *The subject* (what the message is about);
- *The body of the message.*

You can also send a copy (or a blind copy) of your message to another address. Often, you can attach a file. The manual for the e-mail program you are using will advise you on how to use these options.

The fun part comes after you've got all your "message ducks" lined up. Press the *send* command and, whoosh! . . . away it goes!

How Can I Send My Resume and Cover Letter Online?

New and easier methods are appearing almost daily. Most people use one of the following approaches.

The Basic Method

1. First, compose your resume (and/or cover letter) offline, using a word processing program with spell-checking and other helpful features. Take enough time to do a first-class, thoughtful job. Save your resume in your word processor file.
2. Convert your resume to ASCII plain text. Your word processor manual will tell you how.
3. "Import" your resume into an outgoing e-mail message and send it. You can do this by using your software's "copy and paste" feature to enter the text into your e-mail. Or you can "attach a file" to your e-mail message.
4. Read up on the finer technical points of sending e-mail and files; they are discussed in most online guides.

A Deluxe but Iffy Method

The alternative presentation of your resume is more complex and requires more skill, software, and time. If you want your resume to arrive looking much like your paper resume, with formatting, boldface type, various type fonts, and other graphic niceties, you'll have to send not an ASCII file, but a binary file, which accommodates more than plain text. It may require encoding and decoding—if it goes across the Internet. In addition, you must know that the recipient has a word processing program that can recreate your resume as you sent it.

Most people use the one-language-fits-all ASCII resume, even though it isn't as attractive as a word processing resume that is formatted and has other attractive graphic features. Everybody (every computer) can read ASCII.

You may post only your resume online, or you may choose to send a cover letter with it. When you are posting only your resume to a BBS, online resume database, or informal place, you normally would not include a cover letter; in replying to job recruitment postings, you should enclose a cover letter that relates your qualifications to the job's specifications.

Two Ways to Post Your Resume

Basically, there are two different ways to post your resume online.

1. **Upload your resume, using the file transfer feature of your communications software.**
   Follow the directions in your communications software manual to send an ASCII file or a binary file. If you are sending your resume over an online service to a recipient on the same online service (say, from CompuServe to CompuServe), or from your computer to a bulletin board you've dialed into directly, the ASCII or binary file alone is enough.
   If you are sending it across the Internet, you must encode the binary file, using a program like *uuencode* (see the NetNote, "Terms to Know").

2. **Send your resume via e-mail.**
   Read the manual of the e-mail program you're using. Some e-mail programs let you send binary files, but others allow only ASCII text files. Still others allow you to send more than one file in a single message; they can accommodate a resume paired with a cover letter.
   Some e-mail systems allow you to mail a file (resume) as a separate item along with a message (cover letter). Some do not.
   If you want to attach additional portfolio material with graphics, you will have to send it as an encoded binary file. First, make sure the person on the other end can receive a binary file.

How Can I Make Sure the Image of My Resume Looks Good When It Is Received?

Word processing programs (such as WordPerfect and Word) have special formatting codes that allow your resume to be as decorative as you wish, with various type fonts and underlining, italics, and boldface.

By contrast, the ASCII format, a universal language every computer understands, only prints plain text—no variety of fonts, underlining, italics, or boldface. Capital letters, white space and indentation can be used to create an attractive image.

Human eyes may judge the resume prepared in WordPerfect in Figure 7–1 to be superior to the same plain text ASCII resume in Figure 7–2, but job computers do not. Job computers like plain text.

For a full explanation of how to prepare computer-friendly resumes, read *Electronic Resume Revolution* (Wiley, 1993).

CONFIDENTIAL

Martha Kelly Talbot
3501 Bedford Circle
Bend, Oregon 92000
717-234-5678

Seasoned, high energy, versatile manager. Solid track record in customer relations, computer service and operations management. Negotiations and management skills recognized and rewarded.

*   *Established and successfully managed national operations of $125M customer service division of $325M international computer company.*
*   *From start up, through growth of company continually accepted new challenges and contributed to corporate profitability.*
*   *Established and managed a major account program which generated in excess of $6M per year in new account business.*

Management Style: People say I have a unique ability to spot a problem, evaluate a situation and act decisively. My innate intelligence, quick learning capacity and high level of flexibility make me easily adaptable to new situations, products and people. *I keep my eyes on the job* using organizational and motivational skills to get it done . . . on time and within budget. I'm best in culture where honesty is the best policy and customer satisfaction is the goal.

SIGNIFICANT ACCOMPLISHMENTS

*   *Designed and implemented national program for inspection and certification for use computer equipment covering more than 100,000 units.*
*   *Developed and coordinated the procedure and scheduling of all customer engineers technical training; resulting in the training of more than 250 professionals.*
*   *Managed transition from corporate fleet to national automobile reimbursement program; two year project resulted in the elimination of more than 300 corporate vehicles, with a savings of $1M.*
*   *Demonstrated proven leadership skills when entire staff accepted relocation from Southern California to establish new headquarters in Dallas, Texas.*

Figure 7–1   Formatted Resume (WordPerfect)

CONFIDENTIAL

Martha Kelly Talbot
3501 Bedford Circle
Bend, Oregon 92000
717-234-5678

Seasoned, high energy, versatile manager. Solid track record in customer relations, computer service and operations management. Negotiations and management skills recognized and rewarded.

- Established and successfully managed national operations of $125M customer service division of $325M international computer company.
- From start up, through growth of company continually accepted new challenges and contributed to corporate profitability.
- Established and managed a major account program which generated in excess of $6M per year in new account business.

Management Style: People say I have a unique ability to spot a problem, evaluate a situation and act decisively. My innate intelligence, quick learning capacity and high level of flexibility make me easily adaptable to new situations, products and people. I keep my eyes on the job using organizational and motivational skills to get it done . . . on time and within budget. I'm best in culture where honesty is the best policy and customer satisfaction is the goal.

SIGNIFICANT ACCOMPLISHMENTS

- Designed and implemented national program for inspection and certification for use computer equipment covering more than 100,000 units.
- Developed and coordinated the procedure and scheduling of all customer engineers technical training; resulting in the training of more than 250 professionals.
- Managed transition from corporate fleet to national automobile reimbursement program; two year project resulted in the elimination of more than 300 corporate vehicles, with a savings of $1M.
- Demonstrated proven leadership skills when entire staff accepted relocation from Southern California to establish new headquarters in Dallas, Texas.

Figure 7–2   ASCII Resume (Plain Text)

Any employer technically sophisticated enough to be receiving resumes online is reasonably likely to be using an automated applicant tracking system (a job computer) to screen and store your resume.

To keep it simple, if you want your resume to arrive in a handsome format, rather than a plain ASCII format, your best bet is to fax it or postal mail it.

How Do I Prepare a Plain ASCII Text File Using a Communications Program?

1. Create the message using a word processor (such as WordPerfect or Word). As you prepare the file, make sure the lines of text are no more than 65 characters long, to prevent the bulletin board system (or other recipient of your post) from automatically wrapping the text to the next line. Put a space at the start of each blank line between paragraphs. (Pressing the Enter key on a blank line may return you to the message editing menu.)

2. When you are satisfied with the way your resume text looks, save it as plain ASCII text, without any special characters or formatting.

Note that the techniques of saving in ASCII text vary by word processor. ASCII may be known as "nondocument mode" or "unformatted" text, depending on your word processor. Look it up in your word processor's manual.

3. To upload the ASCII text to a bulletin board, log in to the board and go to the message menu.

Follow the bulletin board's directions. The process is similar for other destinations, such as newsgroups and the resources of online information services.

4. In a common scenario, from the bulletin board's message menu, for the recipient and subject, select or type the following:

   All
   Resume posting

5. Rather than simply typing in the information at the standard message text prompt, upload your resume. Tell your communications program you want to start an upload.

Many BBS programs use a command called "U" that uploads messages as files. On most Dos-based and on some Windows-based communications programs, you start uploading by pressing the Page Up key on your keyboard. On Macintosh and Windows programs, you click on the appropriate "Send a Text File" option. Read the manual for your communications program to check specific details on how to start an upload.

6. Depending on the BBS, you will see either the Message Edit menu, or the next available line for the message. You can save or edit your resume with the BBS's standard message editing commands, customize it by typing in additional information related to a specific job opening, or upload a cover letter stored in a different file.

Tip: When you want to know exactly how your resume and cover letter will look to the recipient, upload your documents to yourself first and make appropriate changes. It's almost like cooking—taste, then adjust the seasoning as needed.

The above directions give you the baby-steps method of zapping your resume around the Net. If you need more help, read the excellent *Using Computer Bulletin Boards,* Third Edition, by John Hedtke. (See the Appendix.) Methods of uploading resumes that require special programs are noted in Chapter 8.

What If I Have Only an E-Mail Address from a Commercial Online Service and I Need to Send It to an Employer on a Different Network?

All major online services now have—or soon will have—Internet connections. You can send e-mail and ASCII files from any one to any other. Just use the recipient's address. As mentioned earlier, you can't send a binary file from one online service to another without encoding the file with special programs. You can, however, send a binary file within your own online service without encoding it. When the binary file moves around the Internet, it requires special coding and decoding.

A fine book on this subject is *The Internet by E-Mail* by Clay Shirky. (See the Appendix.)

How Do I Take Advantage of a Listserv (a type of mailing list on the Internet)?

A Listserv discussion group may be a fountain of job news even if it isn't overtly job focused. To subscribe and unsubscribe, see Chapter 4 (Net-Note: "Using Mailing Lists").

How Can I Send the Same Resume to Several Places without Entering and Posting Each One Separately?

You can use a special program, such as one of those mentioned in Chapter 8, or you can do it the standard way.

For example, to post to multiple newsgroups—also known as "cross-posting"—send your resume only once to all the appropriate newsgroups—Newsgroups: [header line], leave one blank space after the colon, followed by the newsgroups' names separated by commas without spaces. As an example:

Newsgroup: dc.jobs,ba.jobs.offered,misc.jobs.offered

What If I Can't Find Something I Want on the Internet?

Scott Yanoff at the University of Wisconsin in Milwaukee has posted instructions about how to find things you may want. Called the *Internet Services List,* Yanoff's resource explains where to find a range of free databases. Nurses can find resources on nursing research, practice, education, and publications, for instance, and somewhere in there, job talk is likely to occur. The Internet Services List is available in several ways:

To access by e-mail:

inetlist@aug3.augsburg.edu

To access by ftp:

csd.uwm.edu
/pub/inet.services.txt

To access by World Wide Web:

http://www.csd.uwm.edu/Mirror/inet.services.html

How Can I Be Sure My Resume Doesn't Fall into the Wrong Hands?

If you're looking for a new job and your boss is peering over your shoulder, the last thing you want is to have your resume flash to his or her attention.

You can't be 100 percent sure the worst won't happen, but you can be 99 percent sure if you practice safe sending.

As one Netter expresses it, there are a couple of ways to "send blind resumes, so employers can't see you're gonna ditch 'em."

Undoubtedly, more blind-remailer services will become established within a year or two. Here's what has turned up so far:

1. **Send your resume through an anonymous server**

   An anonymous server is free, and it provides a front for sending mail messages (i.e., resumes) without identifying you as their source. As you send your first message to the server, which often is a computer resting in a hall of academia somewhere, it automatically gives you a user-identification handle. You are notified of the handle and all subsequent dealings are done through it.

   Example of a handle: an123456@anon.penet.fi

   After stripping your resume of identifying headers, your name, and other giveaway information, you send it to the anonymous server, which redirects it to any number of recipients you specify. When replies come in, they also are sent to the server and are redirected to your original, real address.

   Any reply is anonymized, so the server provides a double-blind, unless the employer chooses to reveal the identity and contact information. Theoretically, you and the employer could dance around for several e-mail exchanges before knowing who the other party really is.

   The anonymous server most people told me about is located in Finland and began as a way for singles and people seeking sex therapy to communicate.

   This approach is not for a crash job search; there may be delays of a few days as the server turns around your resume. Server postings expire after a couple of weeks. If you decide to try the Finland anonymous server for blind resume postings, remember to renew from time to time. Send a test resume before trying the real thing.

   To get more information send e-mail to:

   help@anon.penet.fi

2. **Send your resume through a representative of Help-Wanted USA**

   Accessed through America Online or the Internet, many Help-Wanted USA representatives, for a fee, offer a confidentiality option that will protect your identity and put your resume in the Worldwide Resume Talent Bank. Employer interest will be passed on to you. For details and referral to a representative, contact:

   Gonyea and Associates, Inc.
   1151 Maravista Drive
   New Port Richey, FL 34655
   Internet: careerdoc@aol.com

3. **Try the global job market**
   When you want confidentiality in the international job market, you can send your resume, for a small fee, through:

   OnLine Solutions, Inc.
   1584 Rt22B
   Morrisonville, NY 12962
   CareerPro1@aol.com

What Do I Do When I Am Absolutely Stuck in a Menu or Other Feature and Can't Get Out?

When in doubt, log out. If nothing works, first try pressing the Esc (escape) key. Nothing happens?

Try pressing Control-C. No? Try Control-]. Sometimes Control-XXX works. No luck? Try q or Q (for quit) or the word "exit" or "bye."

When all else fails, log off and exit your communications program. As a last resort, turn your modem and PC off and worry later about getting out.

NetNote

Terms to Know

ASCII Pronounced "askee," an abbreviation for American Standard Code for Information Interchange. A universal code most personal computers understand. (See the Glossary.)

binary file A file that can combine text and graphics—and more. Binary files may include audio, and many word processing files, such as WordPerfect or Microsoft Word. To travel the Internet, binary files must be "encoded" (doctored up in a technical manner) by the sender, and decoded by the receiver. Several encoding software programs are available free over the Internet; use Archie to find them.

uudecode (Unix-to-Unix Decode) A program that lets you reconstruct binary data that were encoded with a uuencode program.

uuencode (Unix-to-Unix Encode) A program that encodes binary data for sending over the Internet.

8 Put Your Job Search on Autopilot

The impatient or thrifty job hunter can turn to a variety of high octane shortcuts—from macros to offline readers. Will one of these e-helpers make you more efficient at finding a job?

"FETCH, MACRO!"

MAKE IT EASY ON YOURSELF

Which do you prefer?

1. To do 10 minutes of repetitive keyboard aerobics as you check out what's new on the job scene.

    or

    To do just a few keystrokes and mouse clicks as you race to useful job market information.

2. To dawdle online as connect-time charges soar.

    or

    To automate offline as a cost-cutting strategy.

If you're like me, you'll want to save time and money. By using autopilots, such as the electronic helpers described in this chapter, you'll certainly pare down your time, and you may be able to cut your monthly charges by more than half.

WHAT AUTOPILOTS DO

Instead of logging in or logging out manually and trying to remember too many annoying little commands, you can accelerate the process by using a *macro* or *script.*

With the help of a *front-end program,* you select in advance the places on the Internet where you wish to go, and the actions you want to take once you're there. Perhaps your wish is to read all new messages, such as all new job postings for marketing specialists. Or perhaps you'd rather read all new messages only in certain sections, such as all new job postings for marketing specialists in the food and beverage industries.

Offline readers let you quickly "grab" the info you want online, get it into your own computer, and mull it over later.

Other autopilots are advanced *communications programs* that zip your resumes along e-mail routes. The communications software used in my office is enhanced with macros and scripts, making it a snap for me to whisk my newspaper column along telephone lines to the Los Angeles Times Syndicate.

Besides saving you money, these inspired creations free you to spend less time on technical online chores and more time on finding jobs, posting resumes, informally chatting in your career field, and sending and receiving e-mail.

NetNote

Types of Autopilots

To keep your learning process simple, types of autopilots described in this chapter are clustered in one of five categories to give you a quick idea of their benefits, even though some can fit in more than one category. Here are the five categories, arranged by relationships, not alphabetically:

Macro   A series of menu selections, keystrokes, or commands that have been recorded and assigned a "keystroke code" —such as "Alt F5." When those two keys are pressed, the macro leaps into action, performing a series of tricks from beginning to end. A single keystroke may cause 20 or 30 steps to occur.

Script   A software program that, like a shorter macro, makes computer things happen like magic. Many people write their own scripts. But some autopilots offer canned scripts.

Front-end program   Software that operates on your computer to provide an interface (connection) with a network or service that "front ends" an operating system. In an analogy to electricity, the front end is like the plug you push in the wall; you never need to know how the electricity flows behind the wall.

Offline reader   A software program that allows you to log off quickly from an online connection as soon as you've received your mail or news. You then read your mail and news on your schedule and respond at your convenience. This saves money because you're not tied to a ticking meter. When you respond through an offline reader, you can use low-cost, nighttime telephone rates or hook-up charges.

Communications program   Software that manages the exchange of data between computers. You can think of it as a "back-end" program. Just as a front-end program works before you do your computer work creating your message, a communications program sends your finished work on its way.

SETTING UP YOUR AUTOPILOTS

A few of the autopilots are free, others have a price tag, usually between $25 and $50, but ranging up to $150 or so. If you are technically adept, you should be able to install any of them.

If you are a novice, consider enlisting the aid of a technically skilled friend, perhaps bartering a home-cooked dinner or theater tickets in return for assistance.

If you can't think of one friend who can help you out, hire a computer coach to install the autopilot and tutor you in the operating routines. Computer whiz students in high school and college generally earn between $4.25 and $10 an hour for tutoring; older computer coaches command between $10 and $40 an hour.

Among the ways you can find computer tutors: by asking at computer stores, high school counseling offices (try the counseling secretary), college career service offices, and vocational-technical schools; by reading or placing small ads in newspapers and computer publications; by contacting a local computer club; by attending local computer fairs.

When your computer guru explains the autopilot's operating routines, write them down on a cheatsheet; if you're like me, you will underlearn and overforget.

Some autopilots described here are products of the big online information services; others are marketed by third-party entrepreneurs, either as shareware or as commercial products.

This autopilot chapter was inspired by my own frustrations when trying to move quickly around the Net. By no means are the products that follow the only autopilots on the market, but they are a sampling of the quality electronic aides available today that can substantially streamline your Net search. Prices noted are vendors'; street prices may be less.

To avoid being repetitive in listing shortcuts that you're likely to find out about on your own, we do not identify certain autopilots that automatically come as part of a package when you sign up with an online service, such as America Online's "FlashSessions." AOL, or an AOL book, will mention the quick moves the FlashSessions feature makes possible.

The autopilots below are listed not alphabetically, but grouped more or less by category in this order: script, front-end, offline reader, and communications programs. Note that autopilots often have feet in more than one camp, making any categorization imperfect.

America Online Whale Express

What It Does

Whalex (contraction of Whale Express) is a script program. It is not simple in construction, but it offers users a very simple way to automate their activities on America Online. It sends and receives e-mail and does a number of other tricks. Example: You can customize a script to search job databases only for certain types of jobs, send Whalex out like a "robo-retriever" to grab only those jobs, and read them offline at your leisure.

Technology

IBM-compatible PC, Windows.

Comments

You can use some of the canned Whalex scripts as is, or you can substantially customize them to fit your needs. Why the name Whale Express? Internally at America Online, the Windows version of America Online, WAOL, is pronounced "whale." Whale Express was created by Bill Pytlovany, one of the designers of the original America Online software.

What It Costs

$39.95 registration fee.

Where You Get It

Third-party product; not officially supported by AOL.

You can receive Whalex in two ways: (1) on disk through postal mail, or (2) by downloading a trial version through AOL. You can use the trial version (shareware) for free until you decide whether it's worthwhile to purchase the registered version.

> Tartan Software
> 143 Horstman Drive.
> Scotia, NY 12302
> Telephone: 518-372-3990
> America Online: tartan
> Internet: tartan@aol.com

1. *Follow these steps* to download from the AOL opening screen; click*
    Go to
2. *Select*
    Computing & Software
3. *In the Computing & Software window, double-click*
    Windows
4. *In Windows Forum window, double click*
    Software Libraries
5. *In Software Libraries window, scroll to and double click*
    Windows AOL Add-ons

* These instructions are for Version 2.0. Downloading Instructions for subsequent versions may vary.

6. *In AOL Add-ons window, highlight and click*
    Whalex

7. *Select icon*
    Download Now

The registered version of Whalex will be e-mailed to you upon receipt of the registration fee.

CompuServe Navigator

What It Does

Navigator, a script program, automates the time you spend on CompuServe in e-mail and in forums where you can pick up career information. It reduces connect time by quickly retrieving and sending messages, files, and resumes. You plan ahead by preparing a script—when the billing clock is not running—in which you select the CompuServe services you will use, and decide the tasks to perform in each service. You then run your script and review the information you retrieve.

Technology

IBM-compatible PC, Windows; also, Macintosh.

Comments

As one Navigator user says, "Autopilots are complex programs and it takes a while to get them configured [set up] to fit your exact requirements and personal choices of online actions. But it's not rocket science and if you read the manual, you should be able to get any autopilot working for you." Support help is available if you get in a jam, including the CSNav-Win Support Forum (Go CSnavsup), which is staffed by CompuServe customer service representatives.

What It Costs

$50 for a complete software kit that includes a $25 CompuServe usage credit.

Where You Get It

1. *Follow these steps* to download from the CompuServe Information Service's opening page; click menu bar's*
    Traffic Light

---

* These instructions are for Version 1.01. Downloading Instructions for subsequent versions may vary.

2. *In typing space, type*
   CSNAV

3. *From Go window, click*
   ok

4. *In CServe Navigator window, move the highlight to and click*
   Download Navigator version (highest number version)

5. *Click*
   Select button

6. *In Alert Window, click*
   Proceed button

7. *In CServe Navigator window, highlight*
   Download Navigator version (highest number version)

8. *Click*
   Select button

9. *From download Navigator version 1.01 window, highlight*
   Download Disk 1

10. *From same screen menu, click*
    Select button

11. *At terminal emulation window, when asked if you want to download it, type*
    Y; press enter

12. *When asked if you want to call the file "Disk 1.Exe," select*
    ok

13. *Receive program.*

14. *From download Navigator version 1.01 window, highlight*
    Download Disk 2.

15. *From same screen menu, click*
    Select button

16. *At terminal emulation screen, when asked if you want to download it,* type
    Y; press enter key

17. *When asked if you want to call file Disk 2.Exe, select*
    ok

18. *Receive program.*
    For customer assistance, call 800-848-8990.

Delphi D-Lite

What It Does

D-Lite is a popular front end, with a strong offline message feature, for Delphi and Usenet groups. This shareware dramatically cuts down on online costs by reading and responding to e-mail offline. It includes many convenience features such as full-screen editing and automatic downloading of multiple files. (*Downloading* is computer lingo for transferring a file from a remote computer to your computer. *Uploading* is the opposite.)

Technology

IBM-compatible PC, Windows or Dos; also Macintosh.

Comments

A SIG (special interest group) on Delphi supports this program. Ted Goff, the cartoonist for this book, describes it as a "natural tool for someone wanting to follow informal job postings on the newsgroups."

Goff explains that he uses D-Lite to do a keyword search for the few messages of interest to him. "I can set it to log in to Delphi, go to the Internet newsgroups I specify, download all the new messages, then log off. This is all automatic—the text scrolls by on the screen so fast that you can't read it. Then, offline, I can do a keyword search for 'cartoon,' 'magazine,' 'newsletter,' and so forth, to find the five messages out of 1,000 that I want to read."

What It Costs

Shareware: $29 registration fee.

Where You Get It

Third-party product; not officially supported by Delphi.

It can be obtained by disk through postal mail, or downloaded. If you order a disk, you must pay in advance and it is not returnable. By contrast, if you download the program, you have 30 days to try it out for free before deciding whether you want to keep it and pay for it.

> Circular Logic
> P.O. Box 162
> Skippack, PA 19474
> Telephone: 610-584-0300
> Fax: 610-584-1038
> Internet: Perry@Delphi.com

1. *Follow these steps* to download from Delphi's main menu; type*
   Computing Groups
2. *From Computing Groups screen, type*
   D-Lite support SIG
3. *From D-Lite support SIG window, type*
   Databases (files)
4. *Type one of the following choices*
   PC version (or) Mac version (or) Windows
5. *Type*
   Read (and download)
6. *Select*
   Down
7. *Receive program. Save in your computer.*

GEnie PC Aladdin

What It Does

Aladdin, a front end, helps you get on GEnie and look around once you're there. It's a powerful software program using menus and screens to automate access to and use of the GEnie services. You can use its easy access features to go directly to specific areas, such as e-mail or discussion groups. You can create and edit messages offline and send them all together in a batch of mail. You can retrieve information from GEnie and store it for later use offline. The offline messaging ability saves you money.

Technology

IBM-compatible PCs, Dos.

Comments

Aladdin can be very helpful in sorting through the information you want in career-related topics. You can do a quick start by reading a six-page guide (*Starting.Doc*). If you're a glutton for punishment, you can go for the entire 90-page manual (*Aladdin.Doc*). You download both to your computer.

What It Costs

Free; a commercial program distributed by GEnie.

---

* These instructions are for Version 2.04. Downloading Instructions for subsequent versions may vary.

Where You Get It

1. *Follow these steps to download from GEnie home screen menu bar; select*

   Online

2. *From next pop-up menu, highlight and click*

   Move to page/ keyword

3. *From next window, type*

   110

4. *From same window, select and click*

   Move button

5. *From the menu Navigator window, highlight and double-click*

   Download latest Aladdin version

6. *From terminal window, type*

   D

   Enter

7. *Receive program. Save in your computer.*

E-Mail Connection

What It Does

E-Mail Connection, an offline reader, is an all-in-one e-mail package that works with CompuServe, Prodigy, and MCI mail. What about the Internet, America Online, GEnie, AT&T, and automated faxing? E-Mail Connection links you to all those services and others, using your choice of CompuServe, Prodigy, or MCI as gateways. The routing is built in, making communication much less nerve wracking. This software not only integrates mail services, but automates mail messaging as well.

Technology

IBM-compatible PC, Windows.

Comments

A computer magazine review of the product says it is "unique, immensely useful and the best e-mail integrator ever." This book's chief technical reviewer, Steve Eisenberg, gives E-Mail Connection "five stars."

What It Costs

$49.95

* These instructions are for Version 1.72. Downloading Instructions for subsequent versions may vary.

Where You Get It

ConnectSoft
11130 N.E. 33rd Place, Suite 250
Bellevue, WA 98004
Telephone: 206-827-6467, ext. 458
Internet: techsupp@adonnis.com

Eudora

What It Does

Eudora is an offline e-mail reader with lots of extras. For direct Internet access, Eudora software allows PCs and Macintosh systems to fully communicate with each other. Direct access may be for T-1 lines or SLIP. With an easy-to-use, menu-based interface, it supports e-mail communication via modem. Eudora allows you to automate your mail and deal with it offline. When you choose to print your e-mail, the Eudora presentation looks superb. A feature-rich software, Eudora makes it possible for you to attach resumes from other programs to messages, provided the recipient also has Eudora.

Technology

IBM-compatible PC, Windows, and Macintosh.

Comments

Susan Estrada, an Internet expert, who is an adviser for this book, highly recommends Eudora as a way to tame the Internet. "Eudora software takes you straight to the Net through a universal e-mail system, which means you don't have to buy a lot of special gateway programs. E for Eudora, E for easy," says Estrada.

What It Costs

$65.

Where You Get It

Computer and software stores, Internet service providers, or order from:

Qualcomm
6455 Lusk Boulevard
San Diego, CA 92121
Voice: 800-2-Eudora
Internet: eudora-sales@qualcomm.com

MKS Internet Anywhere

What It Does

MKS Internet Anywhere, an offline reader, is a good answer to Internet mail and news for the traveling professional and the home and remote office user. In addition to handling thousands of news articles daily—perhaps doing offline research on companies where you'd like to work or do business—Internet Anywhere allows you to set up your own private news and mail networks among friends—ideal for recruiters who want to keep in touch with a candidate pool.

Technology

IBM-compatible PC, Windows, Hayes-compatible modem. Requires a UUCP (Unix-to-Unix Copy Protocol; for Unix, see the Glossary) connection, which you can get from an Internet service provider. The software package includes a book listing more than 100 service providers who offer a UUCP connection.

Comments

MKS Internet Anywhere is based on UUCP store-and-forward technology, which means the network stores your e-mail and news until you call for the information. Many small organizations and individuals prefer store-and-forward networks because they are inexpensive (they don't require dedicated online links). The downloading and uploading of information are scheduled by you for a time when you aren't using your telephone line. It can all happen late at night while you are sleeping. Suppose you wanted to "broadcast e-mail" your resume to 500 prospective employers; this could be a low cost and fairly easy way to do it.

What It Costs

$149.

Where You Get It

Computer and software stores, or order from:

> MKS Inc.
> 185 Columbia Street West, Unipark 3
> Waterloo, Ontario
> Canada, N2L 5Z5
> Telephone: 800-265-2797 (United States and Canada) 519-884-2251
> Internet: sales@mks.com

Off-Line Xpress

What It Does

This software program, abbreviated OLX, is an offline reader for most independent bulletin boards. OLX works like a charm with QmodemPro, a communications program (described below). In OLX you can compose messages that are to be sent via bulletin board.

Technology

IBM-compatible PC, Dos, or Windows.

Comments

OXL and QmodemPro are two of Steve Eisenberg's favorite autopilots. "I like them used as a team. The versatility and easy touch of the point-and-click connections and macros are great."

What It Costs

$40.

Where You Get It

> Mustang Software, Inc.
> 6200 Lake Ming Road
> Bakersfield, CA 93306
> Telephone:800-999-9619
> Fax: 805 873-2599
> Internet: info@mustang.com

Prodigy Bulletin Board Reader

What It Does

Bulletin Board Reader is another offline reader that allows you to automate your interactions with the bulletin boards on Prodigy and to save money by getting your act together offline.

Technology

IBM-compatible PC, Windows.

Comments

This program was created by Dan Lee, outside of the scope of his employment by Prodigy. Lee notes that in Version 2.0 of Bulletin Board Reader, your responses can be uploaded using macros, which in themselves are nifty little time savers.

What It Costs

Freeware (no charge).

Where You Get It

Third-party program; not officially supported by Prodigy

1. *To download from the Prodigy opening screen, "Highlights"; move cursor to and double-click*
    Computers
2. *From next screen, move cursor and double-click*
    Downloads
3. *At Downloads window, highlight and double click*
    Utility Downloads
4. *From the Utilities for Prodigy Software window, move cursor and click*
    Library
5. *At the Library window, move cursor to the tool bar (bottom of the screen) and move to the next page by clicking*
    ▶ (forward symbol)
6. *Move cursor and click on box*
    4-Prodigy Bulletin Board Offline Reader for Windows
7. *Move cursor to bottom of screen and click*
    Download button
8. *From Download screen, move cursor and click*
    Begin download button
9. *Receive file in your computer.*

QmodemPro for Windows

What It Does

QmodemPro for Windows is an advanced communications program—the first to incorporate fax, data, and certain graphics features in the same program. This powerful software comes with lots of macros and features that allow you to assign your own macros to different keys. If you're really revved up about bulletin boarding, you can even use it to set up a mini board of your own, by using the *host* (a program used for a small-scale BBS) QmodemPro script. This may be of interest to recruiters, and to those who wish to start an online "job club," in which members trade job search information and offer mutual support.

Technology

IBM-compatible PC, Windows.

Comments

This software won the 1994 Dvorak Telecommunications Award for Outstanding Telecommunications Technology, which is like an Oscar from the bulletin board industry; Dvorak is a guru on personal computing concerns. This is high praise indeed, but neophytes will need a shepherd to maximize its help in weaving in and out of bulletin boards and other Net nooks and crannies. Dos aficionados may want to use QmodemPro for Dos.

What It Costs

Windows version: $99.

Where You Get It

Mustang Software, Inc.; for contact information see above (Off-Line Xpress).

Procomm Plus

What It Does

Procomm Plus, an advanced communications program, began with a Dos-based version, which grew up to become the world's best selling communications software. Now it has a dramatically good version for Windows users, which, in its notable bag of tricks, allows you to completely automate your resume distribution. For example, in setting up a resume distribution list, you can automate the dialing directory and instruct the program to keep calling until a connection is reached (to a limit of 99 attempts) and your resume finds its destination. You can keep track of call history information to use in reconciling your telephone bills. You can attach "notes" to each resume to help you remember where you got the name of the prospective employer.

Technology

IBM-compatible PC, Windows and Dos.

Comments

Ed Guevara, a technical associate for this book, roots for the Windows version; the author is most familiar with the Dos version. Both are good, but, admittedly, the Windows version does more special things.

What It Costs

Manufacturer's suggested retail: Dos $129, Windows $179. Special promotional pricing and upgrades are available when ordering from DataStorm.

Where You Get It

Computer and software stores, or from

> DataStorm Technologies, Inc.
> P.O. Box 1471
> Columbia, MO 65205
> Telephone: 314-443-3282
> Fax: 314-875-0595
> e-mail: 7370.1100@compuserve.com

PORTABLE ELECTRONIC DOCUMENTS: THE NEXT GENERATION IN ONLINE RESUMES

As discussed in the previous chapter, most resumes are sent online in plain ASCII format, not in a nice, spacey format with an attractive layout.

For all practical purposes, until recently, if you wanted to put a formatted resume into the hands of an employer, it usually meant sending it by postal mail. You could fax, of course, but usually that means long-distance calls to shabby-looking thermal-paper printouts.

Now there's a new development: portable electronic documents (PED). The technology takes the first step toward making sending formatted resumes online a breeze.

PEDs use software programs that allow you to transform your resume/cover letter into files that can go anywhere (hence the adjective "portable"). Once you've turned your resume into a PED, you can use the Internet and commercial online services as your distribution channels. Most PED software works equally well with either IBM-compatible PCs running Windows, or Macintoshes. Here are several questions and answers to expand your understanding.

Q. Can my resume be "saved" in format?

A. Yes. Suppose you prepare your resume in a word processing program such as Word, or WordPerfect for Windows. Next, in your Windows application, you select the PED software as your printer. This causes the resume, with its formatting intact, to be saved in a special file. The formatted file is now ready to distribute.

NetNote

The Finishing Touches

When files roam around the Net, they're often compressed—squeezed together to get more bang for the bits. Because of this compression, after you have downloaded programs, you may need to "expand" them to make them run on your computer.

To clarify, compressed files are, in a sense, "dehydrated" to conserve disk space and to make the transfer time faster. To run a compressed file, the idea is somewhat like the need to inflate a kid's rubber ducky before it will float. Uninflated, the ducky will sink; unexpanded, the programs won't function. To expand some programs, you must apply a separate decompression utility program.

But, praise be, some files are self-expanding. (If you insist on being a purist about it, the real word is "self-extracting.") With this type of file, whenever you see a Dos prompt on your screen, type the file name and it will self-extract. Suppose, for instance, you leave a word processing program to go into Dos; the first blank screen you see may have only a Dos prompt that looks like this: c:\ >.

Here are the relevant definitions for the compression-expansion screen scene:

> **compressed file**   A file (that contains one or more files) that has been squashed to minimize the storage space required. For Dos files, the most common title for a compressed file is .zip. Suppose your file name is "Steve." If Steve became compressed, it would be "Steve.zip." If Steve is a self-extracting file—that is, if Steve can, on his own, get himself out of a tight spot—the file name becomes "Steve. exe."
>
> Comparable extension titles for Macintosh files are "Steve.sit" and, if self-extracting, "Steve.sea."

> **file compression utility**   A program that compresses and/or decompresses files. These utilities often are used to decompress files that have been downloaded from a bulletin board system (BBS). You can download the file compression utility itself from most BBSes. Or, you can buy it as shareware at a software store.
>
> Two popular programs are Pkzip (compresses) and Pkunzip (decompresses); both utilities are contained in the file titled *Pkz204g.exe,* produced by:
>
> Pkware,Inc.
> 9025 N. Deerwood Drive

NetNote (cont.)

Brown Deer, WI 53223
Telephone: 414-354-8699
Fax: 414-354-8559
BBS: 414-354-8670

A comparable Macintosh utility program to compact (compress and decompress) files and reduce e-mail transmission time is StuffIt in the 3.0 version (or newer). It is produced by:

Aladdin Systems, Inc.
165 Westridge Drive
Watsonville, CA 95076
Telephone: 408-761-6200
Fax: 408-761-6206
E-mail: aladdin@well.com

self-extracting file   A file that will self-expand when you run it. You don't have to fiddle with a file compression utility to expand it.

Q. Can my resume letter be printed in format?

A. Yes. An employer is able to print your formatted document from the PED file. It doesn't matter what kind of word processing program the employer is using, as long as the employer has Windows on an IBM-compatible machine, or a Macintosh to view the resume. Further, the employer is not required to have PED software to read your formatted resume.

Q. How do I actually send my PED resume?

A. Upload (send from your computer) your resume to the appropriate file libraries on America Online, CompuServe, Prodigy, Delphi, BBSes, and especially to ftp sites across the Internet. Dozens of anonymous ftp sites allow you to place files online for free. Look for subdirectories called "/upload" or "/incoming." You can use e-mail to notify target employers where to find your resume.

Q. Does this mean I cannot just send my PED resume across the Internet directly to a specific employer?

A. Unfortunately, yes. At this time, when you want to cross the Internet (as opposed to traveling from point to point on the same online service), you must stash your resume in file libraries. An exception to this extra step would be when you transmit within the same online service.

Q. Where is PED software available and how much does it cost?

A. The costs below are sticker prices; street prices may be less.

PED Software

New entries and upgraded versions of portable electronic documents are sure to show up. These are the leaders in the market at press time.

Adobe Acrobat
Version 2.0 $199 for the basic part

Acrobat is powerful. It allows you to view, print, and share documents with both Mac and IBM users. Acrobat can handle Postscript typefaces, the kind used in Macintosh systems and high-end IBM desktop publishing. (You still order either the Windows or the Mac version.) Acrobat comes in three parts: (1) Reader, (2) Exchange, and (3) Distiller. For this book, we are concerned only with Reader and Exchange to transport resume/cover letters. (Distiller, which is more costly, converts typefaces and handles graphics superbly.) The Reader part is free and can be downloaded by any employer to read your resume.

Adobe Systems
P.O. Box 7900
Mountain View, CA 94039
Voice: 800-872-3623

NetNote

Resumes: Just One Face of PED Power

PEDs were really designed for electronic publishing ventures, making instant, full-color, worldwide publishing a reality. Resumes are but one facet of the PED capability.

Remark, a software-add on product (Windows; Macintosh) allows Acrobat users to read, edit and comment electronically on draft PED documents. Employers, for example, can use Remark on PED resumes to easily highlight useful experience, make quick voice summaries, and attach short notes with comments. It is an annotation tool. Single user copies cost less than $130. Remark is a product of Software Partners, Inc. of Mountain View, California (415-428-0160).

Common Ground
Version 2.0 for Windows $150

This is one of the easiest fully featured PED packages to use. For resume sending, it does everything its competitors do. (Desktop publishers will like the Zenographics ZScript that comes as part of the bundle.) Common Ground has good documentation (instructions). A Mac version is due soon.

No Hands Software,Inc.
1301 Shoreway Road
Belmont, CA 94002
Voice: 415-802-5800
e-mail: nohands@netcom.com

WordPerfect Envoy
Version 1.0 $199

A newcomer, Envoy is a delight. It has all the features of the others and some extra features for general business use.

WordPerfect
1555 North Technology Way
Orem, UT 84057
Voice:800-451-5151

Replica
Version 1.0 $99

Replica is aimed at average business users and offers optional password protection. Recipients of protected resumes must enter passwords to view them. If you prefer, you can attach a Replica viewer (reader) to your resume so it can be read. You can try Replica for free by downloading a trial version that allows you to share five fully formatted Windows documents with anyone. This would be a good introduction to PED technology.

Download a copy of REPWIN.EXE from:

        ftp.farallon.com/pub/replica

Farallon Computing, Inc.
2470 Mariner Square Loop
Alameda, CA 94501
Voice: 510-814-5000
e-mail: farallon@farallon.com

Recommendations

Acrobat and Envoy are outstanding products that offer the features for electronic publishing that most companies need. For job seekers, however, Replica or Common Ground is a more affordable solution that will ensure that your resume/cover letter travels well.

—Reporter for this chapter: Steve Eisenberg

EXIT THIS CHAPTER

Did this book overlook your favorite autopilot? In the new dimension of online job search, trying to keep tabs on all the new wrinkles and products is like trying to count grains of sand in a sandstorm. Feel free to help out (e-mail me at jlk@sunfeatures.com), but be sure to describe how your autopilot is special, and exactly what it does for job hunters.

9 Job Finding Strategies and Savvy Moves

Managing your work and life in ways new to our times puts you in front of the competition. Here are a few bonus points to make you a frequent winner.

TRY KEYWORDS FOR SKILLS SEARCHING

What can you do when you've searched job database after job database and still haven't found a decent job lead? The next step is to change your approach and try "skills searching," says Martin Kimeldorf of Tumwater, Washington. Kimeldorf is an educator, author, careers expert, and adviser to this book. What a good idea he has, and what follows is based on Kimeldorf's work.

For an example of skills searching, Kimeldorf chose the career of *teaching*.

"The first thing to realize is that you are not limited to looking for a job as a teacher, but are looking for a job requiring such talents as *organizing, training,* or *communication,"* the career expert explains. "Ask yourself, 'What if I were not selling myself as a teacher, but as a trainer or curriculum developer? What kinds of jobs match my skills, rather than my previous job titles'?"

Kimeldorf calls this concept a **skills-synonym search.**

"You begin to see yourself, not so much in terms of a specific job title, but as a collection of many talents which can be packaged or repackaged to create new career possibilities. This is an extremely important mindset when one hunts in a 'plug-and-play' labor market populated by a large number of people who constantly have to change jobs," Kimeldorf says.

Wishing to test his ideas, Kimeldorf recently communicated online with a New Jersey resident, Stephanie. A former special education teacher who had been out of the job market for several years and who didn't know the "current jargon," Stephanie was persuaded to keep an online log of her research and networking experiences.

After five months, Stephanie reported that Kimeldorf's skills-synonym methods not only helped to clarify her job search goals, but resulted in her landing a new job in a consulting firm that, under contract, provides testing in public schools.

Two more of Kimeldorf's real life examples illustrate how to use the Net to network, job hunt, and research on a "skills" basis. The first example describes the experiences of Thelma, a beginning teacher; the second, of Lois, an experienced teacher. Kimeldorf met both professionals online. He doesn't yet know the outcome of their job searches.

Thelma, a Newcomer to Teaching

Having just earned her teaching certificate, Thelma sought work as a high school English teacher. Thelma began by searching with two words, "English teacher." Because she used two words, her computer took a long time to find all the jobs that used both "English" and "teacher." Only three listings turned up.

NetNote

Read First, Search Later

Martin Kimeldorf recommends that you review online job ads before you start your search. This preparation opens your eyes to what's wanted by employers, thus suggesting new keywords for your resume. In addition, you can better identify the keywords you should use when you search the online job ads.

Next, Thelma tried a broader search on the single word "Teacher." This search produced 32 jobs advertised for substitutes, bilingual educators, counselors, computer support staff, math teachers, and something called "conflict resolution teacher."

Next, Thelma tried searching on an even more general word, "Education." The database produced a whopping 586 entries, but it was not the jackpot she had first supposed. Thelma found many jobs have the word "education" in them because they list the level of "education" required of applicants.

Thelma decided to try another database that also lists job openings by occupational category. In this database, she found various listings in the teaching, education, and training categories, including an opening for a college adjunct art instructor, and a trainer for a computer manufacturer. Thelma thanked Kimeldorf for the skills-synonym, which had widened her horizons.

Lois, an Experienced Teacher

After teaching for a dozen years, Lois had gained the reputation of being a master teacher in her field of English. She had never worked outside the public schools. Most of her jobs were found by word of mouth or by reading teacher job-listing publications. Kimeldorf (screen name: MartinKim) and Lois chatted online. Here's the conversation about skills-synonym searching.

MartinKim	Begin by asking yourself: What skills do I use and enjoy now? What are some words I could list?
Lois	Teaching, education, technology, reading, administration.
MartinKim	That's a good start. But if you search for jobs using words like "trainer," "education," "presenter," "lecturer," and "instructor," you'll be surprised at what you may

	find. Taking a broader perspective helps you to find other jobs, such as those belonging to nonprofits and industry, as well as government.
Lois	I understand. Can you think of any other ways skills-synonym searching could be used online?
MartinKim	Do the reverse. Look in resume databases. Search with keywords to find talented people who may be willing to share knowledge. To test my idea about this, I went into a database and searched for "sculpture." I found one artist. But instead of asking him about sculpting, I sent an e-mail message asking a noncompetitive question: "I'm a sculptor in Tumwater, Washington. Do you know of anyone I might contact to learn more about projects in Washington"? (I would not have asked the artist about sculpting projects in his locale—he would want those for himself.) And he responded—with a lead.
Lois	I see; you are gleaning contacts with this reverse skills-synonym technique. Terrific idea! But back to the job listings. What if the ones I want are old?
MartinKim	Any help-wanted ad, print or online, can be old, and some are for jobs where people are already chosen. Even so, no job lead is dead—until the employer is. Some alert job seekers even revisit job ads six months to a year old, recognizing that turnover is a factor and that the original hire may not have worked out. Time to go. I'm out of here. Happy hunting, Lois.

Skills Searching Can Work in Any Field

Although teaching was used in Kimeldorf's examples because it's easy to explain, you can apply the same principles to your own job search, no matter what you do for a living. What are your skills? What are their synonyms, or their smaller definable parts?

MISS CYBERMANNERS SEZ . . .

In computer lingo, there are some wowzie-dowzie words, like *whatis string* and *go4gw daemon*.

There's even a word for good manners:

Network + etiquette = netiquette

Get it? This means friendly user, rather than just user friendly.

Actually, the delightfully correct columnist Miss Manners does have a fan club on the Internet. If she were advising chipheads today, she'd be the first to say that there are unwritten, though usually observed, rules of netiquette.

As with everything that involves people, in cyberspace too, manners are the lubricant that allows rubbing shoulders without cracking clavicles.

Netiquette Clues

Remember that you are writing (talking) to *people*. Treat them on the Internet with the same courtesy you would in face-to-face conversation. You can hide behind an impersonal coat of virtual armor, but remember that, as a job seeker or recruiter, you want to look as good in the electronic mists of anticipation as you do in the flesh. Here's how that advice translates to your Net messages and responses:

- **Keep up a spiffy appearance**
  Check your spelling, grammar, and punctuation before posting. You may be tempted to write in a stream-of-consciousness style, but those reading your message aren't likely to appreciate it or to perceive you as a clear thinker.

- **Avoid the ammunition dump**
  Even when you are infuriated, bite your mouse! Never insult or demean another network user. If you do, you are a *flamer*. There's a good chance that more than a few episodes of flaming will draw attention to you as a lout. Employers don't go out of their way to hire louts.

  If you find yourself on the receiving end—the flamee—don't let it ruin your day. Head for the Valium and chill out. What can the flamer do—burn up your birthday? Try not to repeat the offense, but if you're new to the Net, being flamed a time or two is inevitable.

- **Speak sotto voice**
  Don't use all capital letters. It's shouting. You don't want to get the reputation of being a LOUDMOUTH.

- **Cut to the chase**
  Keep your job search communication brief and to the point. Organize your thoughts and present them with clarity in your word choice and your format.

As for your marketing materials, one page for a cover letter is O.K. Here's a benchmark for resumes.

New graduates	*One page*
Most people	*One to two pages*
Senior executives	*Two to three pages*

- **Forget cutesy**

  Smileys are also called emoticons—a combo of *"emotions"* and *"icons."* An emoticon is to computers what "Have a good day!" is to the outside world. These little smiling-sad-winking character-like icons (denoted by punctuation marks; see below) must be read with the paper held sideways to be understood. Lots of people think they're adorable.

  Wherever else you may choose to use them, don't let even a hint of an emoticon appear on your resumes, cover letters, or any job-related correspondence. Emotions are not professional in a job search. Your use of a smiley may cause an employer to wonder whether you're a Peter Pan who has never grown up.

Cutesy Smileys

:-)	Happy face
;-)	Wink
:-(	Frown
:-o	Surprise
:-p	Sticking out your tongue

Besides avoiding smileys, it's not a great idea to use common Internet abbreviations in your job search, such as BTW for "by the way" or IMHO for "in my humble opinion." If you ignore this advice and sneak in a smiley or an abbreviation on your cover letter, don't be surprised if Miss Cybermanners bids you TTFN ("Ta-ta for now").

HOW MUCH BAGGAGE SHOULD YOUR E-MAIL CARRY?

Some message senders and receivers boomerang the identical words back and forth so frequently the ensuing messages are repeated for time eternal. This is the forwarding-and-appending (F&A) convention. An example of four messages using the F&A convention is given in Figure 9–1.

Should you use the F&A convention when communicating with employers? It depends. If you're one of hundreds of candidates, it may be expedient to append your answer to the employer's message when you

---

Message 1

Date: Mon, 17 Oct 1995 13:17:13 -700 (PDT)
From: Joyce Kennedy < jlk@sunfeatures.com >
To: John Doe < jdoe@ajax.com >
Subject: Newsgroup Researcher position

Thanks for your interest. Can you describe more about your research skills?

—Joyce Kennedy

Message 2

Date: Tue, 18 Oct 1995 15:27:22 -700 (PDT)
From: John Doe < jdoe@ajax.com >
To: Joyce Kennedy < jlk@sunfeatures.com >
Subject: Re: Newsgroup Researcher position

On Mon, 17 Oct 1995, Joyce Kennedy wrote:

> Thanks for your interest. Can you describe more about your research skills?
>
> —Joyce Kennedy
>
>

My research skills include two years' employment in Caldonia Public Library as an online libarian. I am experienced in using all forms of online tools, which includes everything from gopher to WWW.

—John Doe

Message 3

Date: Wed, 19 Oct 1995 07:52:90 -700 (PDT)
From: Joyce Kennedy < jlk@sunfeatures.com >
To: John Doe < jdoe@ajax.com >
Subject: Re: Newsgroup Researcher position

On Tue, 18 Oct 1995, John Doe wrote:

> On Mon, 17 Oct 1995, Joyce Kennedy wrote:
>
> > Thanks for your interest. Can you describe more about your research skills?
> >
> > —Joyce Kennedy
> >
> >
>

Figure 9–1   Four Messages in Forwarding-and-Appending (F&A) Convention

> My research skills include two years' employment in Caldonia Public Library as an online
> libarian. I am experienced in using all forms of online tools, which includes everything
> from gopher to WWW.
>
> —John Doe
>
>

You appear to have solid online experience. Are you accustomed to using Mac or IBM?

—Joyce Kennedy

Message 4

Date: Thu, 20 Oct 1995 08:43:06 -700 (PDT)
From: John Doe < jdoe@ajax.com >
To: Joyce Kennedy < jlk@sunfeatures.com >
Subject: Re: Newsgroup Researcher position

On Wed, 19 Oct 1995, Joyce Kennedy wrote:

> On Tue, 18 Oct 1995, John Doe wrote:
>
> > On Mon, 17 Oct 1995, Joyce Kennedy wrote:
> >
> > > Thanks for your interest. Can you describe more about your research skills?
> > >
> > > —Joyce Kennedy
> > >
> > >
> >
> > My research skills include two years' employment in Caldonia Public Library as an
> > online libarian. I am experienced in using all forms of online tools, which includes
> > everything from gopher to WWW.
> >
> > —John Doe
> >
> >
>
> You appear to have solid online experience. Are you accustomed to using Mac or IBM?
>
> —Joyce Kennedy
>
>

I can use both systems and have no preference.

—John Doe

Figure 9–1 (Continued)

Message 1

Date: Mon, 17 Oct 1995 13:17:13 -700 (PDT)
From: Joyce Kennedy < jlk@sunfeatures.com >
To: John Doe < jdoe@ajax.com >
Subject: Newsgroup Researcher position

Thanks for your interest. Can you describe more about your research skills?

—Joyce Kennedy

Message 2

Date: Tue, 18 Oct 1995 15:27:22 -700 (PDT)
From: John Doe < jdoe@ajax.com >
To: Joyce Kennedy < jlk@sunfeatures.com >
Subject: Re: Newsgroup Researcher position

You asked about my research skills. They include two years' employment in Caldonia Public Library as an online libarian. I am experienced in using all forms of online tools, which includes everything from gopher to WWW.

—John Doe

Message 3

Date: Wed, 19 Oct 1995 07:52:90 -700 (PDT)
From: Joyce Kennedy < jlk@sunfeatures.com >
To: John Doe < jdoe@ajax.com >
Subject: Re: Newsgroup Researcher position

You appear to have solid online experience. Are you accustomed to using Mac or IBM?

—Joyce Kennedy

Message 4

Date: Thu, 20 Oct 1995 08:43:06 -700 (PDT)
From: John Doe < jdoe@ajax.com >
To: Joyce Kennedy < jlk@sunfeatures.com >
Subject: Re: Newsgroup Researcher position

To answer your question about my facility with Mac or IBM, I can use both equally well.

—John Doe

Figure 9–2   Streamlined Version of Four Messages

respond. If a prospective employer initiates the F&A approach to communications, follow the employer's lead. It will show that you understand the convention and are willing to play by the employer's rules.

When you use the F&A method, be sure your response is distinct from the text of the message forwarded.

Be aware, however, that even in business communication, some employers consider the F&A approach to be tedious and a waste of paper, not to mention hard to read. Instead, these employers prefer that you paraphrase their questions and provide your response, as in the example shown in Figure 9–2.

What if the employer makes the first move and you do not know which approach is preferred? My advice is to use the F&A approach. When the employer responds with message 3, you'll know what to do for message 4.

What if there is no message 3? Get on the telephone and follow up. You've got the best reason in the world to weigh in with a telephone call:

> *I wasn't sure you received my message, and knowing how computers can take a coffee break (a little humor here), I realized I'd better give you a call because I'm very interested in the position we're discussing. Is this a good time for me to flesh out my qualifications, or would you rather set a time to meet?*

As the use of e-mail in job search becomes more familiar, the rules will become clearer. Until then, use your best judgment on a case-by-case basis.

HOT STRATEGY: AIM FOR GAZELLES

Aim for the "gazelles"—the rapidly bounding companies that have up to 5,000 employees and are giving American business a make-over.

If these dynamic companies that started small and grew large quickly continue to go great guns, they'll change the face of tomorrow's corporate America, says one of the country's top trackers of business demographics.

"Large or small"? you ask. According to David Birch's most recent privately published study, "Who's Creating Jobs," small and large firms created about the same number of new jobs, but large firms lost more than they added and small firms added more than they lost—making smaller firms the net creator of all jobs.

But size is not the issue, insists Dr. Birch, president of Cognetics Inc., a Boston economic research firm that studied data from about 9 million companies. Your goal is to identify the hot shots.

The 270,000 gazelles make up only 3 percent of the nation's companies, but they added more than 4 million jobs between 1989 and 1993, a time when fewer than half a million were created overall. (The economy lost 3.5 million jobs during that period, leaving a net gain of only .5 million jobs.)

Particularly impressive, explains Dr. Birch, are the larger gazelles—those on the low end of big, in the 500-5,000 employee range. They never become gigantic, and that can be an advantage. A 400,000-person behemoth cannot change direction quickly, but a gazelle can turn on a dime when it senses opportunity. Three computer companies—AST, Gateway and Dell—have all landed in the Fortune 500 companies recently and none has yet employed more than 5,000 people.

Gazelles are found in any industry, Dr. Birch notes, from water transportation and leather products to lettuce growing and fish wholesaling. The economist says, "Innovation is occurring everywhere in the U.S. economy, not just in certain hot sectors."

Although most gazelles start small, the few that started from a larger base have a truly spectacular record for adding new jobs to the economy. These superstars began their growth with more than 100 employees in 1989. Only 3 percent of the gazelles created about 44 percent of gazelle job growth.

Other major trends noted in Dr. Birch's report:

- Service firms dominate growth, although smaller manufacturing firms do very well.
- Younger firms do much better than older firms.
- Jobs created by smaller, growing companies are just as well-paid as jobs created by larger companies.

What will tomorrow bring? Dr. Birch says: "Once the economy selects a direction and heads in it for a while, the larger firms come back into their own, and capitalize upon their size to grab a larger share of the pie. We would thus expect to see large firms begin to grow again, slowly, and smaller firms improve their performance as well.

"On balance, the small-firm share of new jobs created will probably drop from its near-100 percent [track record] over the past four years to something on the order of two-thirds."

Where can you find these gazelles? Dr. Birch expects to make a database of them available in the near future, but specifics were not available at press time.

One more important report from David Birch: "Common wisdom has it that most growing companies are found in the high-tech or bio tech sector," he says. "Not so. We find that most growing companies are in older, more mature sectors, like paper products, chemicals, instruments, rubber and plastics, electronics, banking, insurance, food products, primary metals, and nondurable wholesaling."

MAKE A GAME PLAN

With a multimedia resume, it's entertainment tonight—starring David Coleman of Atlanta (e-mail: 76114.3607@compuserve.com), a "newbiz" marketer and promotion executive. Coleman, who took a hiatus to battle and beat lung cancer, has decided to push his job search beyond the PC and test the traffic on the information highway.

Coleman doesn't stint on effort. Although his multimedia resume isn't appropriate for most people, it is for Coleman because he's in a promotional career field dealing with music, entertainment, and innovative enterprises. His multimedia resume is bursting with graphics, sound, and a voice message ready for an employer's downloading (from several CompuServe forums, including Musicven, BPforum and Multimedia; the file is called Coleman.zip; or, alternately, Mmresu.zip). Employers need Windows 3.1 software to appreciate this type of departure from a cut-and-dried presentation.

Because he wants a standout employer, Coleman aimed to stand out from the crowd. "Most people who solicit resumes online do so in the ASCII text format. I wanted to be unique, so I designed a multi-media computer version of my resume by buying a book on designing .HLP files for Windows [a technology better understood within the context of a technical manual] and taught myself how to do it," Coleman explains.

This innovative job searcher hopes to catch the eye of companies that are pioneering new forms of entertainment—software companies, multimedia producers, CD-ROM publishers, online entertainment corporations, and the like.

The multimedia resume is only one of the cybersmart things Coleman has done. He checks in regularly with electronic job databases and bulletin boards, and chats online with authors like me who can give his search visibility.

The jury isn't in yet on Coleman's search, but with promotion ideas like this, it's not hard to agree with his assessment, "I am confident that using an electronic resume and online services will help me nail down fruitful employment."

David Coleman has what every online job hunter must have—a game plan.

SAMPLE INTERNET GAME PLAN

This section gives you a sample game plan. My thanks go to Donna R. Dolan, a freelance technical writer in Albany, New York, and John E. Schumacher of the State University of New York's Library Automation Implementation Program in Albany, who gave me the idea.

What follows is loosely based on a portion of their article, "Top U.S. Sources for an Online Job Search." in *Database.**

As you read through, bear in mind that you can also use World Wide Web as well as Gopher, Telnet and ftp. To keep it simple, Web directions are not included in this example of an Internet game plan.

1. **Preliminary tasks**

    a. *Know your search terms.* Helpful phrases to search for include:

    employment opportunities

    job announcements

    job listings

    job openings

    job resources

    job vacancies

    labor

    position announcements

    positions available

    resume postings

    staff openings.

    b. *Determine whether the database is searchable.* Often the use of a slash (/) will give you a search prompt, allowing you to cut to the chase by specifying what you're hunting for, such as "marketing job listings," or "accounting positions available." Give it a try.

    c. *Fix a schedule to job shop.* Establish a routine to check your job resources regularly—daily for an urgent search, two or three times a week if you've got a job but mentally have already left it, and once a week if you're just fishing for new opportunities.

* Vol. 17, No. 5, Oct.-Nov. 1994; pp 34-43; published by Online, Inc., Wilton, Connecticut.

The *Chronicle of Higher Education,* for instance, is a plum resource for academic job offerings. The new position announcements are released online every Tuesday, concurrent with the printed publication. Like the admonition of vendors hawking peanuts at ball games, in scouting help-wanted ads, the principle to follow is, "Get 'em while they're fresh!"

d. *Plan to keep good job records.* Just as with traditional job searches, you must organize some system for keeping track of whom you have contacted and where your resume is posted.

e. *Maintain an Internet log of your search.* Career management should be an ongoing process, not just a priority when you are unemployed. **To remind yourself, you can call this record a** *Career Management Net Log.*

- *Review Chapters 3 and 4* of this book, to refresh your memory and help you more easily appreciate the game plan suggestions that follow.

2. **Find a good Gopher server or two that stocks the kind of resources you want.**

You can basically use Gopher in one of three ways. All three require going through a Gopher client (a computer that receives rather than originates data):

a. Go through a public Gopher.

b. Run a Gopher client program through your dial-up account with an Internet service provider.

c. Download a free software program and create your own Gopher client on your computer.

The last two methods permit you to create a "bookmark." If you are running a Gopher client through your access provider, or have set up your own Gopher client, your customized bookmarks are saved in a file. You can use them each time you go gophering.

But if you telnet into a public Gopher, your bookmarks disappear at the end of each session. If you prefer to create your own Gopher client (on a SLIP/PPP account, for instance), you can download a program permitting you to do so via Anonymous ftp. The book by Harley Hahn and Rick Stout, *The Internet Complete Reference,* described in the Appendix, has a helpful discussion on this point if you need more help.

NetNote

Your Very Own Bookmark

The bookmark feature available to use with Gopher and other client server software, is a handy dandy piece of technology that job seekers will love, once they get the hang of it.

Making your own bookmark is like setting up a speed dialing feature on your telephone. You find great resources and record them. Every time you want to cruise for a job hunt, you can avoid the interminable burrowing through screen after screen of "Gophers around the world," "Gophers of North America," "Gophers of the U.S.," and the like.

When you're ready to hit the job search comet that is the Internet, call up your bookmark, choose the appropriate search function, and you're on your way. Here's how a few lines might look on an abbreviated Gopher bookmark sample (without the techie screen marks) for library job information services:

   a. Jobs and Employment (Rice)
   b. Academe This Week/Chronicle of Higher Education/
   c. College & Research Libraries News Jobs/
   d. Online Career Center (msen.com)/
   e. Online Career Center (Search jobs in Northeast)
   f. Search misc.Jobs.offered article titles

Your Very Own WWW Hotlist

A hotlist is to the World Wide Web as a bookmark is to Gopher. The hotlisting feature gives you the ability to collect favorite places for quick return in later sessions. Related WWW features include *retreat* lists, which allow you to dash back to recent documents within a session, and *keyword search* facilities for sites that permit searching. For details, check an Internet guide.

3. **Find your best discussion groups—mailing lists, particularly Listservs**

   If you have a presence (by subscribing) in the appropriate mailing lists, you'll be in the right place when job openings are announced. They'll come floating through your computer screen.

   But there's a downside to subscribing to every list in sight: your e-mailbox will bulge at the seams. One answer is create an "a" list and a "b" list. You can then choose one of the common ways to handle an overflowing e-mailbox:

- Use two e-mail addresses, directing the "a" list to your preferred mailbox, and the "b" list to a mailbox you open when you have time.

- Subscribe to the "a" list. But seek ways to search the "b" lists without subscribing and cluttering up your mailbox. Whether you can do this usually depends on whether the list is "archived," meaning stored as in a library archive. To determine whether any particular mailing list is archived, send e-mail to the target Listserv *site* address (not to the list address).

To ask, type in the message area:

info database

You'll receive a reply that tells you about archive availability. Be certain to note addresses that you want to use over and over in your customized bookmark.

4. **Find your best Usenet newsgroups**
You do not get e-mail fed back to you automatically and thus you avoid the mailbox-overload problem you may encounter with mailing lists.

Record the most useful newsgroups in your Career Management Net Log. Use the search features of your newsgroup reader software to do the grunt work of visiting your selected groups.

5. **Find your best bulletin boards**
Determine whether a fee is required to participate as a job seeker. Many commercial BBSes charge employers, but do not charge job seekers. Write them down on your Career Management Net Log.

6. **Find your favorite sites on the World Wide Web**
New site locations are sprouting like political signs in an election year. Add the URL (uniform resource locator) addresses to your Career Management Net Log.

7. **Contact employers and recruiters posting job ads**
If you respond to blind ads, you may wish to use the resume confidentiality features discussed in Chapter 7.

When you can determine the postal address, follow up by mailing a paper resume. When you know the fax number, follow up with a faxed resume.

Some people will say this is overkill, but I recommend you err on the side of making sure you get your resume onto the employer's desk. I'm not big on leaving important things to chance.

8. **When appropriate, track down potential employers and start an e-mail professional acquaintanceship**
   Use various Internet location-finding tools, such as *Whois* and *Finger,* to discover e-mail addresses. This strategy skirts secretaries and recruiters who may screen you out before you can meet the person with the power to say, "Yes, I want to hire you."

   Once the e-mail contact is established, you can ask for a face-to-face interview. In the near future, you may be able to use a videophone to talk about your qualifications for employment. Alternatively, soon you'll be able to suggest a videoconferencing, screen-to-screen interview, using more professional equipment.

   On your end, you'll go to a commercial videoconferencing center, probably installed in a copy shop, and rent the equipment for the interview. On the employers' end, a growing number of companies already own or lease videoconferencing operations (see netMCI Business in Chapter 6). The videoconferencing capability is expected to be a standard communication method in businesses before the end of the decade.

   Aldea Publishing's *NetPages* (619-929-1100) gives e-mail addresses in a telephone-like directory of white and yellow pages. The directory is free, but you have to pay mailing costs. As Susan Estrada, publisher of Aldea, says, "If you just can't find the e-mail address you want, the best way is just to call the person's office on the telephone and ask for the correct e-mail address."

9. **Post your resume to appropriate resume databases**
   These may be located on bulletin boards, newsgroups, mailing lists, and the World Wide Web, or on commercial online services.

10. **When appropriate, follow up all serious leads with a telephone call**
    Unless you're pretty sure you're on the short list, you're not going to call London to follow up, just because you e-mailed a resume. But tenacious job seekers make local and selected long-distance calls, checking that "the resume arrived safely." Even in this computer age, the personal touch is effective.

TIPS TO SMOOTH YOUR SEARCH

1. **Define Yourself**
   Don't make the mistake of believing that—without qualification—if you can think it, you can do it. Or that you should do what you love and the money will follow. Reality gets in the way. But discovering what you like to do—and what you're good at— is an appropriate starting point from which to decide the trade-offs you'll accept.

If you haven't sorted this out yet, step back and identify not only what you want to do and where you want to do it, but where your qualifications are most valued. Any number of books are available to help you with this aspect of your career decision, or your job hunt.

2. **Choose to Have the Right Attitude about Computers**
   After writing in my newspaper column about a 39-year-old woman who "hates computers," I received this online note from Dan Sandweiss, who directs career development at Pomona College in Claremont, California.

   "If you read about the types of people that companies seek these days, you will see that this woman is at a great disadvantage. Employers want flexible people who want to learn and who can work with technology. That's the direction the world is going. Often, overcoming the technophobic mindset is more difficult than learning the technology.
   "Many libraries have computers that people can practice on. Most cities and community colleges have introductory classes on using computers. As a person who was mystified about computers some years ago, I can testify that people can become computer literate if they choose to do so."

3. **Watch Where You Post**
   Don't make the mistake of posting your resume in a newsgroup that is designed for job listings. You waste your time, and you annoy the reader.

4. **Heed Employer's Needs**
   Here are several comments from employers seeking to hire on the Internet.

   "After our job posting specifically requesting people with nontechnical backgrounds, we were deluged with resumes from C++ [computer language] programmers. Many people didn't even send a cover letter, just a copy of the resume, leaving us to puzzle out why [these people] thought they were what we are looking for. Needless to say, this is not the best approach to getting a job."

   "Being in the software business, when I advertise online I get people who can find their way around a computer."

"I get the best response by posting late night or early morning on Friday or Saturday. I believe this is due to people coming home and catching up on Usenet over the weekend. Your job posting is more likely to be read if it's near the beginning of 2,000 or so messages."

"The greatest difficulty in online recruiting is staying current with each individual's immediate, usually changed situation. Constantly moving names and addresses from list to list to accommodate altered circumstances is really difficult. We work catch as catch can and hope that the first 10 prospects who write and send a resume contain among them the best, so that we can shut the spigot quickly."

5. **Learn from Others' Success Stories**
Here are two worth retelling:

"I recently completed my MS [master of science degree] at Syracuse University, N.Y., and did my job hunt solely through Internet. The technique I used successfully was to send mail to selected people with the '.com' [short for commercial] extension in their Internet address, such as 'johndoe@hifi.firm.com'. I wrote a small script (see Chapter 8) which waded through postings and extracted the e-mail [addresses] of people with the '.com' extension. I got two job offers this way, including my current one.

I also used newsgroups, Online Career Center, and various online databases, as well as a weekly online newsletter. That also yielded several interviews and a couple of offers. In all, Internet is the best job-hunt resource I found."—*Rahul Bhargava, Milpitas, California.*

"I put my resume up on the World Wide Web and because someone where I now work read it, I ended up getting hired. However, it wasn't simply enough to put my resume up, I had to have some bait. That bait was a Unix program I wrote for converting postscript documents to Web format documents. I cross-linked it to my resume. To see what I mean, take a look at the cross links.

To access my script on the World Wide Web:

http://stasi.bradley.edu/ps2html/ps2html-v2.html

To access my resume on the World Wide Web:

http://stasi.bradley.edu/~guru/resume.html

Because of the Internet, my search has been successful."—
Jerry Whelan, Long Island, New York

6. **Show Your Flag**
Invest the time you need to be certain your resume is deposited in all appropriate resume databases of companies and third-party recruiters who may one day be interested in hiring you. Be sure to update your resume regularly to add new accomplishments or contact information. If confidentiality counts, review the advice in Chapter 7.

Being on display around the clock and around the calendar is true career management.

ARE COMPANIES HIRING INTERNAUTS?

One interesting question turned up from Betsy Schrieber (not her real name) at a Southern university.

"I know someone who found a job in New York City through a local Usenet group. Which reminds me that I am looking for work doing Internet research. Are you aware of the kinds of companies looking for 'Internauts'? Although I do know it is a necessary skill these days, who can use the net surfing skills I have acquired?"

The answer isn't clear, but the use of Internetting competencies as occupational skills is likely to follow the pattern set by computer skills. In the early days, people with computer skills had their pick of jobs, chiefly because few people knew how to use computers. But as the numbers of the knowledgeable grew, computer literacy became somewhat like being bilingual—secondary to primary skills, such as engineering or banking. Today, people are hired for primary skills and simply expected to be computer literate. Exceptions are for jobs requiring substantial knowledge of complex computer science or computer repair.

People with Internet teaching or operative skills today probably have a limited window of opportunity to use them. How long a window? Perhaps a few years, perhaps 10 years. Internetting skills may become as common as driving skills are today.

WHAT'S AHEAD

The implied job agreement of days gone by, the one that traded loyalty for job security, is fading like yesterday's technology.

Being downsized and out is too often a fact of life in a new era of personal portability in employment. The nature of job security itself has changed. The rules of job security today are as follows:

Rule 1.   Make sure your skills are up-to-date and wanted.

Rule 2.   Know where and how to sell those skills.

Rule 3.   Be willing to repeat Rule 1 and Rule 2 again and again.

As companies keep cutting back to fewer core employees, replacing in-house people with outside contractors—the "outsourcing" trend—you can no longer count on long-term promises from even the most substantial corporations. The concept of a contingency and global work force is discussed and implemented on a daily basis.

Some observers even speculate that jobs are no longer the best way to organize work, that the traditional job is headed for history's scrap heap. The argument says that "the job" worked fine in the newly industrial world of the 19th century, but is poorly adapted to a fast-moving, information-based economy.

A natural outgrowth of such philosophies and developments is the notion of the virtual organization, a new style of business arrangement that allows a handful of people in one place to be linked electronically to other workers anywhere in the world. However the future rolls out of the crystal ball, we are in the throes of a workplace revolution in the way human resources are being used—and not being used.

On another front, technology titans are making striking forecasts of the brilliant digital future that awaits us. From interactive TV, which most people agree is not yet ready for prime time, to universal e-mail, to the wireless networks that will change the face of communications in truly amazing ways, there's not much argument that we are experiencing a workplace revolution in tools, as well as in the use of human resources.

What does all this mean to most of us? For starters, do not give up on the traditional job search—yet. We're in a transition of uncertain duration. At the same time, those of us who do not want to find that technology has overtaken our career value will look toward the future, rather than being frozen in the past. It's time to give up being a technophobe.

To paraphrase Mame in Patrick Denni's novel, *Auntie Mame,* "Life is becoming a cyberfeast. And some poor fools are going to starve to death."

When you find it necessary to upgrade your skills, and to market them once again, look for the electronic edge.

MAN HAVING HEART ATTACK SAVED BY E-MAIL

Forget the impact of romance by e-mail, support groups by e-mail, and politicking by e-mail. That's small potatoes compared to the ultimate proof that the electronic dimension has changed our existence forever. Consider the case of Jack Miller, a man whose life was saved by e-mail.

Miller, a management information systems specialist, wasn't feeling well one day last year in his office at Witco Corporation in Woodcliff Lake, New Jersey. He was then overcome with severe chest pains. As he was losing consciousness, Miller punched a few keys on his computer and sent an SOS to coworkers. Like a hospital's code blue, the coworkers came running and administered CPR while waiting for paramedics.

Why didn't Miller just cry out, the ordinary, person-to-person way? He couldn't. He had lost his voice and his ability to breath effectively. From necessity, Miller seized the electronic edge. He typed: "HELP. FEEL SICK. NEED AID."

Your need for new opportunities to earn your way in life may not be life-threatening, but it is certainly career-important. Try the electronic edge yourself. You can log on to a world of job finding resources that may open your future to vistas you never imagined. More people than ever are agreeing that it's time to *hook up and get hired!*

Appendix:
The Scenic Tour

Resources That Show You the Best Ways to Go around the Net

Unless you have a pet technical wizard in your pocket, use books and publications to learn the ins and outs of smoothly moving around the electronic universe.

Some bookstores devote whole wings to the Internet. Libraries are stocked with books on the Net, and a number even employ online librarians to take you by the hand into an environment that someone once compared to New York City without street signs.

Most books will help beginners. For readers who already understand geekspeak, a comprehensive list of current Internet titles is available.

To access the list:

Usenet newsgroup alt.internet.services

Or, receive it via anonymous ftp:

rtfm.mit.edu:/pub/usenet/news.answers/
internet-services/internet-book-list.

Or, receive it via e-mail:

To: mail-server@rtfm.mit.edu
Subject: < subject line is ignored >
Body: send usenet/news.answers/internet-
services/book-list

Here's one more online way to stay current on what's new with the Internet, which may include trends or resources. Read the Internet Monthly Report, available from a number of sources, including Merit.

To access the report by anonymous ftp:

nic.merit.edu < look in the newsletters directory >

In this resource chapter, we start with books listed alphabetically by title, and conclude with print magazines. (Many general Internet guides identify electronic magazines.) Prices are as of press time, as listed by the publishers.

BOOKS

The Complete Idiot's Guide to the Internet
by Peter Kent (Alpha Books/Macmillan Computer Publishing) $19.95

This lighthearted but information-packed guide helps newcomers hook up and find their way around the sprawling Net. The humorous, nontechnical approach includes Speak-Like-a-Geek definitions, E-Z Shortcuts, and Techno-Nerd suggestions.

CompuServe For Dummies
by Wallace Wang (IDG Books) $19.95

This is a one-stop lighthearted explanation of CompuServe, one of the major online information services. Find out how to find career help, shop, play games, join forums, get the latest news, and do research.

Connecting to the Internet
by Susan Estrada (O'Reilly & Associates, Inc.) $15.95

A buyer's guide with substantial technical advice, this is an excellent book for the business, school, or individual seeking practical advice on how to determine the level of Internet service required, how to find local service providers and, how to evaluate the quality and price of their services.

Cruising Online: Larry Magid's Guide to the New Digital Highways
by Lawrence J. Magid (Random House) $25.00

An insider's guide to the best spots on the Internet, Prodigy, CompuServe, and America Online. This volume comes with coupons for hours of free online time on four different services. A good value.

Electronic Resumes for the New Job Market
by Peter D. Weddle (Impact Publications) $11.95

You can conduct a job search 24 hours a day and 365 days a year by producing an electronic resume suitable for today's resume-scanning technology. The author is president of Job Bank USA, a leading electronic resume database company. Working with tens of thousands of e-resumes daily, he is well versed on the topic.

The Elements of E-mail Style:
Communicate Effectively via Electronic Mail
by David Angell and Brent Heslop (Ziff-Davis Press) $12.95

A reference for business communication, this work suggests new rules for English grammar, usage, and composition for the electronic universe. The authors are technical writers who have 10 computer books to their credit.

The Hitchhiker's Guide to the Electronic Highway
by Pamela Kane (MIS Press) $21.95

With entertaining stories and practical advice, you are escorted through the author's analogy to big cities—huge commercial online services like CompuServe, America Online, and Prodigy—and small towns—bulletin board systems (BBSes). You visit libraries ranging from giant commercial databases to special-interest BBSes.

How the Internet Works
by Joshua Eddings (Ziff-Davis Press) $24.95

This full-color book is a graphic feast. The author takes the novice by the hand to explore the vast volumes of information available through the Internet and online services. All the reader needs is curiosity about this massive cybercommunity.

How to Use the Internet
by Mark Butler (Ziff-Davis Press) $17.95

A guide with big, colorful illustrations on every page, and step-by-step directions on how to take advantage of all the Internet has to offer. Users get their bearings in Unix, Internet's operating system. Dozens of tip sheets offer practical advice and troubleshooting hints.

Inside CompuServe
by Richard Wagner (New Riders Publishing) $19.95

This book features CISNAV, a new navigational tool, in a graphical, easy approach to using and navigating CompuServe. A variety of popular software is discussed, including CompuServe Information Manager for Windows. Information is aimed at the typical business and recreational user.

The Internet Companion: A Beginner's Guide to
Global Networking, *Second Edition*
by Tracy LaQuey (Addison-Wesley) $14.95

Beginning Internet users are introduced to the ins and outs of communicating on the Internet. Newbies gain the ability to connect to this vast network of networks, and they try out their new knowledge firsthand.

The Internet Companion Plus, *Second Edition*
by Tracy LaQuey (Addison-Wesley) $19.95

An updating of a popular book that now has an added feature: direct access to the Internet via Delphi, an Internet access provider. Readers learn how to master the language, culture, and etiquette of the Net. A prime choice to start your Net experience.

The Internet Complete Reference
by Harley Hahn/Rick Stout (Osborne McGraw-Hill) $29.95

A total guide by two Internet masters that includes everything from using e-mail to connecting to remote systems via Telnet, and from reading the news to holding live conversations. Includes a vast catalog of more than 750 free Internet resources.

The Internet Direct Connect Kit
by Peter John Harrison (IDG Books) $29.95

Turn your 386- or 486-compatible into a full-fledged Internet node (central computer) with the step-by-step instructions and software contained in this book. The author has assembled a set of tools that will make accessing and using the Net easy for millions of new and current users.

The Internet Directory
by Eric Braun (Fawcett Columbine/Ballantine) $25.00

Recommended by *PC Computing* magazine, this is a book of electronic addresses and descriptions that gives instant access to up-to-the-minute sports scores, news, weather forecasts, and special topics from archaeology to zoology. In addition, it offers access to more than a thousand university and public library catalogs around the world.

The Internet For Dummies
by John Levine/Carol Baroudi (IDG Books) $19.95

A witty and irreverent, but wonderful guide for the beginner, this book's friendly approach cuts through the network jargon with simple references to command, service, and linking basics, thus enabling users to swap e-mail, conversation, and software worldwide with ease.

Internet For Dummies Quick Reference
by John Levine (IDG Books) $8.95

This no-frills, amusing, best-selling guide for beginners is the closest thing to an Internet help button. A reference provides plain-English explanations of terms and basics, what you can get from Internet, how to find stuff, and how to get to it. It is cross-referenced to *The Internet For Dummies*.

The Internet Business Book
by Jill H. Ellsworth and Matthew V. Ellsworth
(John Wiley & Sons) $22.95

Everything you need to know to hop on the Internet and make your cash register ring! This solidly researched work by two ace Internet sleuths should be in every business library.

The Internet by E-Mail
by Clay Shirky (Ziff-Davis Press) $19.95

A book for those who would like to tap the resources of the Internet but can't access the Internet in their area, can't afford to access it, or simply don't want to learn all the protocols of the Internet. E-mail users of MCI Mail, Prodigy, CompuServe, and America Online, and college or business users will find this book very helpful.

Internet Explorer Kit for Macintosh
by Adam C. Engst/William Dickson (Hayden Books) $29.95

This book shows how to use the Internet, taking readers in and out of social groups and special Internet discussions, and sharing all the online customs and jokes. Through a running dialog with other experienced users, the authors use actual screen shots to teach readers how to explore the Internet.

The Internet Guide for New Users
by Daniel P. Dern (McGraw-Hill) $27.95

A highly authoritative but easy-to-read resource for anyone who wants to join, understand, and use the Internet. Dern, a former editor of *Internet World* magazine, has been using and writing about the Net for more than a decade. This work not only shows newcomers how to get up and running, but also provides key information for experienced users. Keep it next to your computer.

The Internet Navigator
by Paul Gilster (John Wiley & Sons) $24.95

A best-selling all-around guide that reveals every facet, from how to locate and deal with service providers to how to send and receive e-mail. The author, an Internet guru, tells how to make the most of limited access—how to use the Internet if your computer is attached via an e-mail-only connection.

The Internet QuickStart
by Mary Ann Pike (Que Publishing) $21.99

A book that explains Internet basics to absolute beginners, this guide offers a series of quick tutorials. Hands-on learning makes navigating the Internet productive, and skill sessions cover topics such as logon, e-mail, database searches, and Internet news.

The Internet Resource Quick Reference
by William Tolhurst (Que Publishing) $17.99

Recommended by *PC Computing* magazine, this work gives readers an indispensable reference to news groups, mailing lists, e-mail, ftp, Gopher, and more—all organized alphabetically to create a user-friendly reference book. It discusses more than 3,000 news groups and mailing lists.

Internet Starter Kit for Macintosh, Second Edition
by Adam C. Engst (Hayden Books) $29.95

This update of a best-seller provides everything Mac users need to connect to and navigate the Internet. Readers learn how to get connected, where to look for what, and how to master e-mail, downloading, and ftp sites. A bonus disk gives powerful utilities for getting online.

The Internet Unleashed
by SAMS Publishing (SAMS/Prentice Hall Computer Publishing) $44.95

This is the big one—an all-in-one authority for the experienced Internet navigator. Packed with advanced techniques for exploiting all the Net tools, it shows inquiring readers how to start and maintain an online media service. A value-added disk features dozens of PC-based Internet tools, along with an updated electronic listing of useful Net resources.

Marketing on the Internet with Mosaic, Lynx, and HTML
by Jill H. Ellsworth and Matthew V. Ellsworth
(John Wiley & Sons) $24.95

Detailed advice on how to incorporate an online multimedia strategy into a marketing plan. Includes everything from getting a business connection on the Internet to creating an effective World Wide Web page.

Mastering the Internet
by Glee Harrah Cady and Pat McGregor (Sybex Inc.) $39.95

A 1,500-word book packed with information for the new Internet navigator as well as the experienced user. In addition to advice for individuals, it contains guidelines for businesses and schools moving onto the Net. Another feature: Tips on creating your own World Wide Web sites and Gopher servers. A comprehensive treatment by two expert Internauts.

MORE Internet For Dummies
by John Levine (IDG Books) $19.95

This expanded guide to "surfing" the world's fastest growing network picks up where its predecessor, *The Internet For Dummies,* left off. The book is full of great Internet tips for all those users who want to know where to go and what to do after getting connected.

Navigating the Internet
by Richard Smith/Mark Gibbs (SAMS Publishing) $29.95

A comprehensive book/disk set that provides users with instant access to e-mail, electronic news services, and free software. With examples and step-by-step instructions, it provides information for joining special-interest discussion groups on topics ranging from PC hardware to bungee jumping.

Netguide
by Peter Rutten/Albert F. Bayers III/Kelly Maloni (Random House) $19.00

As the Internet becomes an entertainment as well as an information medium, a program guide becomes an essential tool. This is it, plus free connect time and free updates.

New Riders' Official Internet Yellow Pages
by Christine Maxwell/C. Jan Grycz (New Riders Publishing) $29.95

An easy reference to the Internet, this volume identifies leads to topics ranging from acting to zoology. It's designed for professionals, researchers, browsers, and explorers. The coverage and detail make this a valuable guide.

The 1995 Internet Business Directory
by Seth Godin/James S. McBride (IDG Books) $26.95

Here's your chance to find out who's doing business on the Net and what services they offer. Organized by specialty, this reference features a brief description as well as the contact address of each company. Valuable coupons are included.

The On-Line Job Search Companion
by James Gonyea (McGraw Hill) $14.95

From the founder of the America Online Career Center and the Internet Career Connection, this book teaches the use of commercial computer network services, online databases, bulletin board services, software and CD-ROM programs, resources on the Internet, and related electronic technologies to change your career direction, post your resume, and connect to thousands of employers and job openings worldwide.

The Original Internet Yellow Pages
by Harley Hahn/Rick Stout (Osborne McGraw-Hill) $27.95

With its telephone book design and easy-to-reference alphabetical format, users get information on what is available on the world's largest network. The huge listing of resources covers well over 100 categories.

Point & Click Internet, *Macintosh edition*
by Seth Godin (Peachpit Press) $12.95

Mac users will like this small book that shows them how to use America Online to get to the Net and move around. The book gives plain-English descriptions of what you must know.

Riding the Internet Highway
by Sharon Fisher (New Riders Publishing) $24.95

With a disk for graphical interface and free connect time, this book focuses on the new Internet users' problems and teaches how to access Internet from online services. It is a resource for e-mail etiquette and procedures, Netnews topics, and reference materials.

Teach Yourself the Internet: Around the World in 21 Days
by Neil Randall (SAMS Publishing) $27.95

This well-organized tutorial can be used by individuals or groups. It takes readers on a global learning expedition in just 21 fun-filled lessons, and provides information on ftp, Archie, and WAIS, to name a few of the zillion topics.

10 Minute Guide to the Internet
by Peter Kent (Alpha Books/Macmillan Computer Publishing) $12.99

In a quick and easy guide to understanding and navigating the Internet, readers follow concise, 10-minute lessons to learn about everything from hardware to e-mail, from downloading files to participating in news groups. The minitutorials are easy to follow and packed with helpful tips, definitions, and troubleshooting advice.

The Traveler's Guide to the Information Highway
by Dylan Tweney (Ziff-Davis Press) $24.95

This book guides trips around today's most popular online services and the Internet. From searching for a specific interest group to making your travel arrangements to sending e-mail, it's a dandy with lots of full-color maps.

Using Computer Bulletin Boards, *Third Edition*
by John V. Hedtke (MIS Press/Henry Holt & Co., Inc.) $29.95

This update of an award-winning book by a leading technical communications consultant introduces novices to computer bulletin board systems, basic telecommunications, and the Internet. Intermediate and advanced BBS users learn highly effective techniques for extending their online reach. The book's very comprehensive coverage is enhanced by a diskette with working copy of the QMODEM 4.5 TestDrive communications package.

Using the Internet
by William A. Tolhurst/Mary Ann Pike/Keith A. Blanton
(Que Publishing) $39.95

A guide that explores the resources and tools of the Internet, this package comes with a disk that includes software to get connected. It covers how the Internet works, gives instructions on transferring files and e-mail, and advises on how to find someone.

What's On the Internet
by Eric Gagnon (Peachpit Press) $19.95

The old saw, "You can't tell the players without a program," couldn't be more accurate than when referring to the Internet. Finding out what newsgroups exist on the Net and what they're like can be overwhelming. This book guides readers to the contents of the Internet's core—its online discussion and information groups. It's well worth the read.

The Whole Internet User's Guide and Catalog
by Ed Krol (O'Reilly & Associates, Inc.) $24.95

Recommended by *PC Computing* magazine and a best-seller, this book is a treasury of online resources. Find databases, carry on discussions with colleagues worldwide, participate in discussion groups, subscribe to electronic journals, and collect free software.

Your Internet Consultant: The FAQs of Online Life
by Kevin M. Savetz (SAMS Publishing) $24.95

FAQs stands for Frequently Asked Questions. The book's Q&A format allows readers to quickly zero in on specific information about a particular subject, or access advice to solve a problem. It contains hundreds of tips, and is filled with practical advice, acceptable for any user level.

Zen and the Art of the Internet: A Beginner's Guide
by Brendan P. Kehoe (Prentice Hall) $23.95

Recommended by *PC Computing* magazine, this friendly, general-overview book is targeted to Net freshmen. It presents fundamental topics often assumed by many network users to be absorbed through osmosis.

PUBLICATIONS

Subscription Contacts

Boardwatch
8500 West Bowles Avenue, Suite 210
Littleton, CO 80123
Telephone: 800-933-6038
E-mail: subscriptions@boardwatch.com

Computer Life
P.O. Box 55878
Boulder, CO 80322
Telephone: 800-926-1578

ComputerWorld
P.O. Box 2043
Marion, OH 43305
Telephone: 800-222-7545
E-mail: 73373,1230@cis.

Connect
Pegasus Press
3487 Braeburn Circle
Ann Arbor, MI 48108
Telephone: 313-973-8825; 800-438-2666
Internet: pegasus@cyberspace.org

Internet Business Advantage
Online Solutions for Business Success
Wentworth Worldwide Media
1866 Colonial Village Lane
P.O. Box 10488
Lancaster, PA 17605
Telephone: 800-638-1639
E-mail: circulation@wentworth.com

Internet Business Journal
Strangelove Internet Enterprises
208 Somerset Street East, Suite A
Ottawa, Ontario
Canada K1N 6V2
Telephone: 613-565-0982
E-mail: at380@freenet.carleton.ca

Internet World
P.O. Box 713
Mt. Morris, IL 61054
Telephone: 800-573-3062

Online Access
900 N. Franklin, Suite 310
Chicago, IL 60610
Telephone: 312-573-1700

Open Computing
McGraw-Hill
P.O. Box 571
Hightstown, NJ 08520
Telephone: 800-257-9402

PC Computing
P.O. Box 58229
Boulder, CO 80322
Telephone: 800-365-2770

PC Novice: Personal Computers in Plain English
120 W. Harvest Drive
Lincoln, NE 68521
Telephone: 800-424-7900
Fax: 402-479-2104

Wired
P.O. Box 191826
San Francisco, CA 94119
Telephone: 800-769-4733
E-mail: subscriptions@wired.com

Note: All computer magazines own e-mail addresses for editorial departments, but not all provide e-mail addresses for subscription departments.

Newspaper Computer Sections
Many newspapers have launched excellent special computer sections. As an example, the *San Diego Union-Tribune's ComputerLink* appears every second week and has an enthusiastic readership.

Free Publications
Local and no-cost computer magazines are found in major cities in computer retail stores, packaging and mailing shops, and deli's. In San Diego, for instance, *ComputerEdge, Computer Journal,* and *Computer Resource* are available to interested readers. In San Francisco, *Computer Currents* and *MicroTimes* are available.

SOFTWARE

The Beginner's Guide to the Internet for Windows
by Patrick Suarez $39.95

Tutorial software. BGI/Win describes all major Internet tools in plain English. The user clicks on colorful icons representing such functions as e-mail and telnet, then clicks through succeeding screens of instruction and example. The interactive program features bright graphics and offers a short quiz at the end. BGI/Win also has a fast search tool that looks through 10,000 newsgroup and mailing list resources to find the resource needed. Updates for newsgroups and mailing lists are posted on the Net.

Suarez Associates
P.O. Box 764
Miamisburg, OH 45343
Telephone 513-323-6121
E-mail: pat@bgi.com

ORGANIZATION

InterNIC

In 1993, the National Science Foundation began funding the Internet Network Information Center (InterNIC). The InterNIC's purpose is to help users get connected to the Net, and, once online, have free access to information about using its resources. You can use searchable Internet "telephone books," resource listings, links to other information sites, and more.

To get general information about the Internet, help in getting connected, or a list of Internet service providers, call the 800 number below.

If you're already on the Net, you can get to the InterNIC files via ftp, Telnet, Gopher, or WWW. There's even an e-mail "infobot" to fire back information, and a general reference desk ("refdesk") e-mail address you can use to send questions directly to information representatives.

Telephone: 800-444-4345

E-mail:

refdesk@is.internic.net

In the body of the message, leave the subject line blank and type

send INDEX

Gopher to:

is.internic.net

Look in:

Top Documents Requested at InterNIC IS

Telnet to:

is.internic.net

Login:

gopher

Ftp to:

is.internic.net

Go to the

infosource/faq subdirectory)

URL: http://www.internic.net

Glossary

Information Highway Terms Made Simple

access   The ability to get information or use a resource by the correct combination of software and hardware.

address   The string of characters that identifies a sender or receiver of messages, a computer site, or the location of a computer file.

Example: president@whitehouse.gov

Much like a street address, an e-mail address is how you reach someone or something. In the not too distant past, e-mail was the only commonly used method to communicate across the Internet. Now there are other options. A URL (uniform resource locator) address is used to reach a resource on the Internet, most often via on the World Wide Web.

anonymous ftp   Anonymous file transfer protocol, also known as anon ftp. Variation of ftp frequently mentioned in Internet literature. A way to transfer copies of the millions of files to or from systems that are open to the public. Offerings include shareware, programs in public domain, books, pictures, sounds, just about anything. With anonymous ftp, you do not need an account (user name and password) to enter a system that's open to the public and "grab" (pull to your computer) the files you want. See also *shareware*.

Archie   A tool for locating files on the Internet via anonymous ftp. Can be used to search all over the world for a specific computer file that is stashed who-knows-where in a pool of nearly two million files. See also *anonymous ftp*.

ASCII   Pronounced "askee"; abbreviation for American Standard Code for Information Interchange, a universal code most personal computers understand. ASCII files are plain vanilla without special formatting codes. To many viewers, these plain text files with no frills are hard to read. Most e-mail for job seekers is sent and received as ASCII messages.

auto-dial   A feature of many communications programs that allows you to preset your modem to automatically dial the telephone number of another computer. Otherwise, you have to manually enter the telephone number each time you dial it.

baud   A measurement of how fast a modem can transmit information over a telephone line from one computer to another. Sometimes used as a synonym for BPS (bits per second), but not exactly the same. Computer buffs say the term *baud* is outdated and BPS is more accurate. Many people have 9600 BPS and 14,400 BPS modems. Some have 28,800 BPS modems. Speeds are heading faster and faster. Generally, the faster the information zips along telephone lines, the cheaper the telephone and network bills.

BBS   Bulletin board system—a communication computer that has one or more modems. Allows people with modem-equipped computers to connect by telephone, or, to enter the Internet, if the BBS has an Internet connection. BBS participants telephone the BBS and swap information, computer files, programs, or stories. An electronic version of a meeting hall where users with common interests exchange information.

binary file   A file of digital information—more than plain text. To look at a binary file on your screen, you must first download it. Binary files can be pictures, word processor documents, executable files or compressed data files. See *download; executable file;* see also Chapter 7.

BPS   Bits per second: the speed of information transmission. Eight bits usually equal one letter, character, or byte. See also *baud*.

byte   A computer storage unit. Holds the equivalent of a single character, such as the letter A, or a dollar sign, or a decimal point. The word *dog* takes three bytes of information.

chat mode   When two or more people are holding a real-time conversation through an online service or bulletin board. The words you type pop up on the screen of the other person or persons, and vice versa. See also *real time*.

click   To make an action happen by selecting an item on a computer screen. Once you move the computer cursor to a particular icon or word, press and release the mouse button. Program directions often say: "Point and click." When nothing happens after one click, try clicking twice.

communications program   The program that controls the transfer of data through a modem to and from another computer. You cannot use a modem to go online without a communications program.

configuration   The combination of the hardware and software components of a computer system; the software settings that customize a system.

connect time   The amount of time a user spends logged on to a computer system or connected to an information service. Charges on connect time can add up to big bills. Make sure you understand the costs up front. Prices vary all over the map. Some services do not charge for connect time.

cybernaut   An expert in the world of computer communications. See also *Internaut.*

cyberspace   A term coined by William Gibson in his futuristic novel *Neuromancer,* in which people connect to the computer network directly by means of their brains. The term has come to refer to all the sites that can be accessed electronically in a large computer network such as the Internet. In general usage it means the "world" of computers and the society that gathers around it.

data   Information—facts or figures—expressed in text, files, databases, sound, or graphics. The data are manipulated, operated on, or processed by, a human or a computer program.

database   A structured collection of electronically stored information—for example, a computerized file of resumes, or a file of job openings. Databases hold large volumes of data and are used to store, organize, and retrieve information. Once entered in a database, records and files can be sorted alphabetically or numerically by fields (the categories you define when you set up the database).

dial-up line   Connection of one computer to another by using the modem of one to dial the telephone number of the other; the opposite of a direct connection. See *PPP, SLIP account,* and *T-1 line.*

digest list   A way of receiving discussion group messages. Messages from individual members are compiled and distributed all at once.

digital   The use of numbers. The word is derived from digit, or finger. Today, digital is synonymous with computer.

discussion group   An electronic "club" of people who like to talk about the same kinds of things—jobs, hobbies, or science. One type of discussion group is a *newsgroup;* another type is a *mailing list,* which may be managed by a computer program known as a listserver. The most common listserver programs are called *Listserv* or *Majordomo.* Not all discussion groups are computer-managed; some are handled by individuals. Either way, a discussion group is a cyberspace salon in which people swap messages.

domain name   A name given to a host computer on the Internet (so other computers can find it). An established hierarchical naming structure for computer addressing on the Internet. Address components are separated by periods (usually called dots). The author's domain reflects the name of her company, Sun Features Inc., which is in a commercial category. Thus it is expressed as "sunfeatures.com" Her complete Internet address is:

jlk@sunfeatures.com

download   To retrieve or receive information (files) from a remote computer. If you upload a file, you transmit a file from your computer to a remote computer. See also *upload*.

e-mail   Abbreviation for electronic mail, a network service that allows you to send and receive messages via computer.

e-mail address   The domain-based address identifying the location of your mailbox. It's where you get your e-mail. See also *domain*.

encryption   Scrambling the contents of a file to ensure its confidentiality. Encryption programs generally require a password to execute encryption and the same password to execute decryption.

executable file   Actual programs you can run on your computer, often available by downloading from the Internet, bulletin boards, and other network services. See *download*.

FAQ   Pronounced "fack"; Frequently Asked Questions. A list of the most commonly asked questions and their answers. They are posted regularly by most network newsgroups and mailing lists to keep newbies from asking the same questions ad infinitum.

file   A segment of computer information identified by a unique name. Sometimes files are within a directory, which may be given as part of the file's complete name.

file server   A central computer used as a storage device for data and programs that all users on a network may access. A reservoir of information to be called up on demand.

File transfer protocol (ftp).   The "rules" that allow users to transfer files (batches of information) between computers.

Finger   A Unix program that may allow you to track down information about a specific Internet user—or identify all the users who are logged in at a particular computer site—if you know the name of the appropriate computer (domain name). Finger is widely used in academia, but not in the commercial sector. Some Internauts shut off the finger feature as a security measure.

flame   Any abusive and angrily sent e-mail message—or posting to a newsgroup—usually containing words better left unsaid. Often a personal attack against the author of a message.

flamers   People who get a reputation for frequently sending flames. Becoming known as a flamer is risky for job seekers because they lose credibility and respect.

forum Virtually the same thing as a conference or newsgroup. An arena for discussions in which members can post and read messages. See *discussion group*.

freenet A free network system that people in a community use to share information and access the Internet.

freeware Free software.

gateway A connection between two online services or networks. A special-purpose gateway computer may allow you to access the Internet, as in gateway service provider. Or, a gateway may only allow two services to exchange e-mail.

Gopher A software tool for boiling everything down to menus from which you make selections. What should you do when you're searching for information but can't remember all the different commands? Gopher solves the problem. This menu-based browsing tool allows you to "go for" publicly available information on the Internet.

Gopherspace All of the thousands of Gopher systems, each operated by different institutions, such as the University of Minnesota, Washington University in St. Louis, and the Cleveland Public Library. Collectively, the resources made available by Gophers are called *Gopherspace.*

GUI Pronounced "gooey"; graphical user interface. The term "user interface" means the tools a computer gives you to boss it around. A graphical user interface gives you graphics (pictures) as tools to use. See *click*.

header In a document, any text appearing at the top of every page. In e-mail, the top portion of a message containing such identifying data as to recipient of message, sender, date and so forth.

hypertext Linking and displaying information in another portion of a document by selecting on highlighted text or icons on a screen. Hypertext is the fundamental basis of the World Wide Web. See also *World Wide Web.*

information highway A term that originally meant running an optical fiber into most homes in the United States, a goal that is at least 10 years off. Commonly, the term, including its contraction, "I-Way," is used to mean what is already happening. As Microsoft CEO Bill Gates says, "When society adopts electronic mail, when a corporation starts electronically circulating resumes and job orders and product orders and schedules, when small business begins using electronic channels to market products, that's the information highway. When you're logged into an online service, plugging into a bulletin board, that's the information highway. When you use your PC to send resumes or do home banking, that's the information highway." Increasingly, writers are using the terms "information highway," "information superhighway," "electronic highway," "data superhighway," "infobahn," "cyberspace," and "the Internet" as synonyms.

interface In software, a program, such as Microsoft Windows, with commands, messages, and codes enabling you to more easily use complex, underlying software programs. See *shell account.*

Internaut An Internet user.

Internet The global network of networks that communicate with each other. These communicating networks are of varying types, such as government, academic, military, organizational, research, and commercial. The trend is for all networks to be gateway-linked (hooked up) to the Internet; this includes long-standing private commercial networks.

Internetter An Internet user, whether expert or novice.

Internet service provider A company that provides connections to the Internet. Another term that means the same thing is *Internet connectivity provider.*

IRC Internet relay chat; an Internet live conference. A kind of party-line chitchat with people everywhere. Often used as a soapbox to publicize an opinion or a mission. Anyone with the right software and with access to an IRC server (computer) can open a channel with a specific name and topic.

ISDN Integrated Services Digital Network; wags say it means *I Still Don't Know.* ISDN is poised to become the preferred Internet access method for individuals and small businesses. A digital telephone service, ISDN eventually may replace modems in providing a superior quality of faster and cheaper graphic, sound, and video files. With ISDN service, the telephone lines to your computer carry digital signals, rather than analog signals. ISDN would be ideal, for instance, in sending an image (picture) of your resume online, rather than just the text. Some telephone companies already offer ISDN telephone lines for less than $30 a month; observers expect ISDN to become commonplace by 1997 or sooner.

kilobyte A measure of the size of a file. A kilobyte consists of 1,024 bytes, each representing a character of text. Referred to in print as KB.

knowbot Knowledge robot, a power information retrieval tool that automatically searches the Internet for specific information.

Listserv One of many programs that manage the creation and distribution of mailing lists. See *discussion groups.*

load   To copy a program or file from disk, tape, or another computer in cyberspace onto your computer. To put a file into a computer program.

login   Your name or identification number and password to hook up to a computer, usually one that is a part of an information service, bulletin board, or Internet gateway provider. When used as a verb, it becomes two words: log in.

login prompt   A system's message on your computer screen that signals you it is ready to accept a login name.

logoff   To disconnect.

lurker   A regular reader of messages who never posts. See *posting*.

macro   A computer shortcut for executing a series of commands or for executing routine commands. Instead of 30 commands, for instance, you can design a macro (preprogram) instructing your computer to do the same thing with many fewer keystrokes. Macros are commonly used in word processing and formatting, spreadsheet, and database programs. The author uses them for login sequencing. For streamlining your work, macros are marvelous time savers.

mail reflector   A special mail address; e-mail sent to a mail reflector address is automatically forwarded to a set of other addresses. Typically used to implement a mail discussion group, but it can be used to protect the identity of a resume's writer.

mailing list   A type of e-mail discussion group. See *discussion group*.

menu   A list of computer program choices presented on a screen; just what it says—electronic dishes to be served up.

merge   A word processing program utility that allows you to print customized form letters by combining lists of variables, such as names and address fields, to be merged with a form letter at designated merge points. A very useful technique for sending out resumes and cover letters.

MIME   *M*ultipurpose *I*nternet *M*ail *E*xtensions, a proposed standard for multimedia mail on the Internet.

modem   Short for *MO*dulator/*DE*Modulator, a piece of computer hardware that acts as an interface between computers and telephone lines, allowing your computer to communicate with other computers. See *ISDN*.

moderated list   A mailing list with message contents that are filtered through a moderator before distribution. The purpose is to improve the quality of information passed to members. Moderated lists are uncommon because moderators are generally not paid and the work is time-consuming. See *discussion group*.

moderator A person who, based on certain criteria, controls the content of articles and messages to be posted or distributed within a moderated newsgroup or mailing list. See *discussion group*.

monitor A video display screen allowing you to see computer information.

Mosaic A graphical interface to the World Wide Web. A tool that allows visual hyperlinks—you see related information you like and jump to it. Example: You're studying resume writing and see an icon representing sample technical resumes, another icon representing sample resumes for liberal arts graduates, and yet another for mature people. If you're an engineer, you'll want to click on the technical resumes. Once there, you may have further options, such as choosing tips from technical recruiters or technical job descriptions. See also *World Wide Web*.

mouse An input device. You can use it instead of a keyboard to give commands to a computer. Mice have one, two, or three buttons. A trackball (like a big rolling marble on a mouse) or a touchpad is preferred by some users. See *click*.

multimedia The combination of one or more forms of communication media, such as text, sound, motion video, still images, graphics, and animation.

net citizen Anyone with a network address.

netiquette A pun on "etiquette." Proper behavior on the Net. Think of Miss Manners in cyberspace.

network Two or more computers that are connected by transmission channels and cables, supporting hardware, and software. Networks come in two varieties: (1) local area networks (LANs), in which all the computers are housed in close proximity, such as in one building; and (2) wide area networks (WANs), in which computers can be located around the city, country, or world.

news reader A software program that allows you to read newsgroup postings.

newsgroup A special-interest group on Usenet, a network in which you can post and read messages. See *discussion group*.

offline Not connected to any computer, information service, or network.

offline reader Software product that allows you to dial into a bulletin board or other system, download a collection of messages, and log off. Offline readers allow you to avoid additional long-distance charges because you can read the messages after you hang up. The readers also let you compose replies or new messages, batch them, and upload them automatically, with similar time and cost savings.

online   Electronically connected by modem or by hardwire to a remote computer, information service, or network.

online help   Screen access to self-help, included in most software packages. Provides information and instructions on using the software, and lists commands or keystrokes to solve your problems.

online information service   An online service, generally provided at a monthly rate that covers a certain amount of free access time or a set number of messages at no additional charge. Extra costs are incurred when you use more time or send more messages than provided for in the standard service package. Online services provide subscribers with access to specialized databanks, including such interactive services as making travel reservations, buying and selling stocks, sending and receiving e-mail, and otherwise conducting business transactions.

password   A secret word or code for a login name that allows access to a computer account. As a rule, you choose your own password. It keeps outsiders from having access to the account.

personal computer   A stand-alone, desktop-type computer likely to be used by an individual or small business.

port   Either the hardware through which data are transmitted (the plugs on the back of a computer) or the number that identifies a particular Internet function or program, such as Telnet or Gopher.

posting or **posts**   As a verb: sending a message to a bulletin board, newsgroup, or other destination online. The message itself is called a post (plural, postings). Two examples: Laura posts a message and she reads job postings. Kenneth is posting and he reads job posts.

PPP   Point-to-point protocol, a protocol that lets a computer communicate directly with other computers on the Internet via telephone lines. Favored by Macintosh dial-up users. See *SLIP* account.

protocol   Rules for how computers will act when they talk to each other.

real time   In computing, an operating mode under which data are received and processed immediately. The results are returned instantaneously. It means right now—not later.

remote   Not in your location; may refer to a computer to which you're connected by modem.

shareware   Programs written by software authors who allow you to try the product before buying it. The software can be downloaded free, but payment is expected from people who want to continue using it. You might say shareware comes wrapped in the honor system. See *download*.

shell   A software interface, such as Microsoft Windows, that stands between you and another computer program, making the other program easier to use. See *interface*.

shell account   A way to use a dial-up account with an Internet service provider. Can be simple menus—or complex Unix commands.

signature   An e-mail feature: a customized complimentary close or sign-off text file, may be appended to the end of e-mail messages. Signature text often identifies the sender by name and contact information.

SLIP account   *S*erial *L*ine *I*nternet *P*rotocol, a protocol that lets a single computer with a telephone line and modem directly use the Internet protocols for virtually any Internet function; in contrast, a shell account offers Internet access only through your gateway provider's computer. In practical terms for job seekers, without a SLIP or PPP account, without downloading files, you can't run Mosaic, which means you can get text, but no pictures or sounds. Without special new software, such as SlipKnot or TIA, your access is only as good as the provider's tools. Bottom line: Most job hunters will need only a shell account (easy), not a SLIP or PPP account (harder).

software   Any set of instructions for a computer. Also known as a program or application. May be issued on floppy disks, compact discs, or online computer files.

subject line   The line of entry supplied by an e-mail sender to describe the contents of the message.

sysop   *sys*tem *op*erator, the person in charge of keeping a computer system up and running. A sysop may honcho a bulletin board system or forum, keeping things humming and maintaining order. Most sysops are volunteers, so be nice.

T-1 line   A high-capacity, direct connection to the Internet. Expensive, but fast and classy.

TCP/IP   Transmission Control Protocol/Internet Protocol. The combination of protocols that allows computers on the Internet to exchange data.

Telnet   A program that enables you to log into other computers from your own networked machine. This valuable program saves long-distance charges if you can log in via a local telephone number.

text file   A file with—surprise!—readable alphanumeric text. See *ASCII*.

thread   A subject of discussion on a message area on a bulletin board or discussion group. The messages in a thread usually have the same subject or topic line at the top, such as "Electronic Resumes." If you're interested in electronic resumes, you can follow the thread of conversation by watching for it in your e-mail.

tree   A hierarchy of newsgroups.

Unix   An operating system developed by AT&T, usually found on large computers. It's the software backbone of the Internet. Because of easy new programs you need not know the Unix commands to navigate the Internet. If you are using Unix, cheatsheets with Unix commands are available; example: to logout on Unix, type Control-d, logout, exit.

unmoderated   A discussion group (newsgroup or mailing list) that does not filter its messages through a moderator before they are posted.

unmoderated list   A mailing list whose messages are not filtered by a moderator before distribution. The most common type of mailing list. Distribution on a moderated list receives higher quality messages because messages are screened for redundant and relevant content, but people on unmoderated lists receive mail fast, allowing for freely flowing discussion.

upload   To send information and/or files from your computer to another computer.

URL   uniform resource locator. Technically, a standard addressing system. In common usage, an Internet address for people who have placed data on the World Wide Web. Example: "What's the URL of E-Span on WWW?"

Usenet   The User's Network; provides news and e-mail. A large, popular, informal collection of computer discussion groups. You can throw out questions in the *appropriate* group; in a job newsgroup, for example—"Does anyone know if sports marketing people are being hired in Minneapolis?"

uudecode   (Unix-to-Unix Decode) A program that lets you reconstruct binary data that were encoded with a uuencode program.

uuencode   (Unix-to-Unix Encode) A program that encodes binary data for sending over the Internet.

Veronica   *Very Easy Rodent-Oriented Netwide Index to Computerized Archives*—a searching service of Gopherspace. See *Gopherspace*.

virtual   Simulated by a computer.

WAIS   *Wide-Area Information Server*, a very powerful, user-friendly system for looking up information in libraries and databases available on the Internet. The search is by keywords.

Windows   The trademark name of Microsoft, Inc., for its powerful, multitask, graphical software interface for Dos-based systems.

Winsock   Electronic "sockets" to the Internet; needed by computers using Windows to run such programs as Mosaic. See *Mosaic*.

wonk   Formerly meant unattractive, boring person; now increasingly used to mean an expert in a subject.

World Wide Web (*WWW* or *W3*)   A fun-to-use service (actually a protocol) that give you freedom to leapfrog from resource to resource on the Internet; a hypertext system that lets you jump from place to place using linkages. To follow a trail of hyperlinks, you pick a topic that interests you and view related information, from which you select another topic that interests you, and so on. You're here, you're there, you're everywhere, like Tarzan swinging from tree to rock to lake. See *hypertext*.

XModem   An older file transfer protocol.

ZModem   A newer and faster file transfer protocol that allows moving batches of data (several files) at one time.

Index